DIVORCE AND REMARRIAGE IN THE BIBLE

by
Kenneth E. Jones

Warner Press, Inc.
Anderson, Indiana

Published by
Warner Press, Inc.
Anderson, Indiana

All scripture passages, unless otherwise indicated, are from the King James Version ©1972 by Thomas Nelson or the Revised Standard Version ©1972 by Thomas Nelson.

Arlo F. Newell, Editor in Chief
Dan Harman, Book Editor
Cover by Larry Stuart

CONTENTS

FOREWORD

Right in the middle of our late 20th century family crisis turmoil comes a world of advice, a staggering accumulation of case studies and ever increasing statistics that tell us that our society is wandering in confusion about the place of marriage in our daily lives.

The church keeps valiantly lifting the Bible standard of one wife for one husband for life. But our heart-ties, our family loves, the day to day practical facts of marriages in trouble make us look with extreme doubt on the ability of modern families to live up to God's plan.

At the heart of any serious search into the solutions for today's family problems is the simple question, "What does the Bible say?" For Bible believing Christians, this is the starting place.

Dr. Kenneth E. Jones has mapped out for us a path that leads to a clearer understanding of God's full intent toward man's family living. Not all of our modern questions are answered. Not all of a local congregation's knotty problems are solved. Indeed, this present book may very well be the forerunner of a second volume that deals with what we are to do in our day with the problems that face us, in the light of what the Bible says.

This present volume is geared toward self-study. But realizing that many of the marriage questions facing today's adults might be better answered in the setting of small group discussions, the publishers have produced an excellent leader's guide authored by Dr. Jones. We recommend it for church groups and other gatherings of those who respect the Bible's authority and light on a most important facet of our modern world.

The Editors

PREFACE

This book began thirty years ago, when I was faced with the problem of counseling a divorced Christian who wanted to know if it would be wrong to remarry. I had never participated in the wedding of one who had been previously married and divorced. But some aspects of this situation forced me to wonder if remarriage could sometimes be acceptable in a Christian. I was forced to go back to study what the Bible said about it. As a result of my study at that time, I wrote down a summary of my conclusions. This summary, with a few minor revisions or additions, is printed as the last chapter of this book.

A few years later, I was asked to lead a conference in a meeting of ministers on the subject of divorce. I did so by reproducing the summary of conclusions I had written down before. With the encouraging response of that group ministers, I used the same material in a later group.

Then, in the fall of 1988, I was asked to lead a conference on the subject in the Indiana State Ministers Meeting. It was suggested that I might want to prepare a manuscript for the group to read and study. Knowing the importance of such a manuscript, I relectantly agreed to do this conference, and prepared a paper which was about half the length of this book. Again this material was well received, and I was urged to do more with the material. It was about this time that Warner Press asked me to expand the manuscript into a book they could publish, and to prepare a leader's guide so that it could be used in groups for Bible study on this vital subject. This I have done.

It was with real reluctance that I began this book, as it is a subject of vital importance to the church, but one which has not usually been systematically studied from a biblical standpoint. There are misconceptions about what the Bible has to say on the subject. There have been some excellent scholarly studies on the subject, but these are not easily available to the average Christian. Some of the books which are widely used have expressed concepts which are hard to support Scripturally.

Not all the problems have been solved here. Much more needs to be written on this subject. Perhaps few will agree with every word written here. But I have done my best, and have written in this book the conclusions to which my study so far has brought me.

Everything has been supported by Scripture, and it has been shown where there is room for difference of interpretation of some passages. My prayer is that it will give the church a sound basis for solving some of the problems involved in marriage, divorce, and remarriage.

Though the book is written as a guide for the layman, it has been necessary to deal with the biblical teaching about pastors and their marriages. It would have been less than complete to omit such passages. Further, almost every Christian has to face sometime in life the fact that some pastors have been themselves involved in divorce, even if only through reading about such things in the newspapers, or hearing about some pastor across town or in another city.

It can be seen from the Bibliography that an attempt has been made to use the best studies others have made of this subject. I am grateful for the scholars who have done this work, and have learned much from them. At the same time, I have done my own study of all the biblical passages, in the original languages, and with all the helps I could obtain. I need to thank the librarians of the Southern Baptist Seminary and Asbury Theological Seminary for helping me use their resources. The latter especially went out of their way to help me do my research.

I am grateful for the pastors and scholars who have read this manuscript in an earlier form: Dr. Milo L. Chapman, Rev. Ernest H.

Gross, Jr., Dr. Sherrill D. Hayes, Dr. Marcus H. Morgan, Dr. Montford L. Neal, and Rev. Marvin S. Sanders. It goes without saying that I, not they, take full responsibility for what is written here, yet I am glad for their input and their encouragement. The hard work of Dan Harman, Warner Press Book Editor, has made this a better book than it would otherwise have been.

May God bless each of you who study this book.

Dr. Kenneth E. Jones
Retired Professor of Bible and Theology
Mid-America Bible College

TWENTY REASONS TO STUDY THIS BOOK

1. It is important for every Christian to know what the Bible teaches about such a vital subject as this.

2. If you are thinking about getting married, this book will help you know what the Bible says about what you are considering.

3. If you are thinking of living with another without being first married, you need to know why the Bible says this is wrong.

4. If you are married, you need to know what the Bible says about the permanence of marriage and how married life should be lived.

5. If you are considering a divorce, you need to search the Scriptures, with the help of this book, and learn what God has to say to you about this step.

6. If you have been divorced, you need to know what the Bible says about how to live the rest of your life.

7. If you have been divorced and are

thinking about being remarried, you need to know whether or not the Bible says God will be pleased with this.

8. If you have been divorced and remarried, you need to know what the Bible says about the rest of your life.

9. If you are a parent, you need to understand what the Bible teaches about marriage so that you can help your children understand about Christian marriage.

10. If you are a teacher, you need to understand clearly so as to teach others the Bible truth about marriage.

11. If you are a pastor, you need to know the truth about what the Bible teaches about your own marriage, so as to make it strong and truly Christian.

12. If you are a pastoral leader, you need to be able to teach others from the Bible what God wants a marriage to be.

13. If you are a pastor or church leader, you need to know how to help others with their marriages.

14. If you are a pastor, you need to know what to do if you are facing the breakup of your own marriage.

15. If you are a pastor, you need to know how to help other pastors in their own marriages.

16. If you are an area administrator, it is imperative for you to understand what the Bible teaches about marriage, divorce, and remarriage.

17. If you make any decisions about minis-

ter's credentials, you must make sure you seek to make Christian decisions about divorced ministers.

18. If you are a member of a congregation, you need to know how to have a Christian marriage yourself and to pray for and with others who are having trouble in their marriage.

19. As a member of a congregation, you need to know how to feel and act if your pastor is facing the breakup of marriage.

20. You ought to know all you can about Bible teaching on marriage, divorce, and remarriage for your own good and for the good of others you may influence.

MODERN PROBLEMS WITH MARRIAGE

We do not have to argue the concept that something is wrong with marriage and family life in the United States today, for it seems to be plain to all of us. If we care about the family, we can see that it is not what it should be. Divorce is all too common, and there are too many troubled families. Further, we can see that children are being hurt by both broken and troubled families.

If we are old enough, we do not need to be told that there have been great changes in family life in the last fifty years. In the twenties and thirties, family life was far different from what it is today. Some of the changes have come about because of changes in society:

a. Change from a rural to an urban country.

b. Change from farm-centered to industrial economy.

c. Change to a much denser population.

These changes in the makeup of our country have had effects on family life all over the country. It is easy to see how the change from rural to an urban society has changed the family. Consider the typical rural family of the twenties. They ate breakfast together, did much of their work together, and always ate the evening meal together. After the work of the day was done, they sat together reading, talking, or playing until bedtime, which was early for two reasons: First, there was no electricity, and so they retired early to save on lamp oil. Second, they got up early so as to do the chores before breakfast. This made it possible to make the most of the daylight hours.

This rural family knew that the only way to have food on the table and clothes on their backs was to work together. Children learned early that they could have nothing without work. (Actually, the so-called Protestant work ethic was not really from Protestant theology but from necessity!)

WAR, TELEVISION, AND TRANSPORTATION

Three other factors have brought about major changes in the family. One was the Second World War. It is not only that so many of our finest young men were killed or seriously wounded in the war itself. But the men who were unable to fight had to work such long hours in the factory, and the women also left the home to work. Some husbands and wives met briefly once or twice a week and never had time to eat together. If they both worked swing shifts, they never seemed to be on the same shift, and so they could do little or nothing together. I remember writing during that time that the family would never again be the same as before. That was more true than I realized.

The second factor was the invention and proliferation of television. TV was invented in the early twenties but was not considered useful for anything, and so it was unknown until the late forties: someone got the bright idea that television could be used to sell the oversupply of goods that the factories were able to turn out following the war. That idea started the ball rolling.

Selling goods is the primary purpose of television. We were told to buy TVs because they could be so helpful in education. But that is not their primary purpose, and never was. Television educates us as to the many things we ought to *buy* if we want to be healthy, wealthy, and happy. If a program does not persuade enough people to buy the products advertised, then it is either radically changed or taken off the air and replaced. This is true whether it is entertainment or news.

Television has changed the way people spend their money. But even more importantly, television has changed the way we spend our time.

What did we do with our evenings before

television? For one thing we talked to one another. We read books. And we visited other families. And when we visited, we talked. Or we children listened to our parents talk and joined in the conversation when we pleased. A wide variety of other people-centered activities filled the evenings: games, work projects, trips to visit friends and outdoor fellowship times. We were a family, and families liked to be together. How times have changed!

The first change came with radio, which was common for a couple of decades before television. But the change was not drastic, for the whole family listened to the radio together while they did other things—sewing, studying, or whatever. One did not look at radio. Television, on the other hand, divides the family. Conversation stops. Everyone sits facing—not one another—the television. Families may even have several sets so each can choose what to watch, and then they are no longer even in the same room. Television has divided families, thus detracting from the force for good which families ought to have on individual development.

Add to the deleterious effect of television itself—the content of television shows—and we see the reason for much of the change in family life today. In the constant attempt to attract viewers, the producers, writers, and actors keep going further and further from what is good and wholesome. Adultery, divorce, and sexual promiscuity are portrayed daily as the accepted thing. Those who watch are bound to be affected. Christians have to control themselves closely if they are to keep their values straight.

The third factor bringing great change in the family is the amazing mobility of our society. This has been brought about by the proliferation of the automobile; each adult has a car, and each teen-ager looks forward to having one as soon as he or she reaches the age at which the state qualifies him/her for a license. So the family members each go a different way, and the whole family may be together only once or twice a week, even for a meal.

CHANGES IN ATTITUDES TOWARD MARRIAGE

There have been great changes in marriage and family over the past half-century, especially in the United States. Marriage was considered to be a commitment, but now there is a great fear of any form of commitment to anyone. Marriage was considered to be for all of life. But now it seems that many do not expect any marriage to last long. My wife and I have been married 48 years, and it is sad to see the amazement which people show when they hear this.

A recent study of the changes in American concepts and moral convictions has not only shown some changes, but has attempted to analyze some of the causes:

Americans believe in love as the basis for enduring relationships. A 1970 survey found that 96 percent of all Americans held to the ideal of two people sharing a life and a home together. When the same question was asked in 1980, the same percentage agreed. Yet when a national sample was asked in 1978 whether "most couples getting married today expect to remain married for the rest of their lives," 60 percent said no (Yankelovich 1981, 103-105).

Love and commitment, it appears, are desirable, but not easy. For, in addition to believing in love, we Americans believe in the self. Indeed . . . there are few criteria for action outside the self. The love that must hold us together is rooted in the vicissitudes of our subjectivity. No wonder we don't believe marriage is easy today . . . But the very sharing that promises to be the fulfillment of love can also threaten the self. The danger is that one will, in sharing too completely with another, lose oneself (Robert Bellah, *Habits of the Heart*, Berkley: University of California Press, 1985, p. 90).

CHANGES IN ATTITUDES TO DIVORCE

There have been corresponding changes in attitudes toward divorce. Divorce once was considered a disgrace. It did not happen often, but when it did, it was to be whispered about. Divorced persons were not to be fully trusted. They might have a hard time, for instance, if they wanted to run for public office.

We can see the changed attitude and the resulting prevalence of divorce today. We see it in the growing divorce rate in this country. It has been pointed out that in certain years divorces have outnumbered marriages. But this is no support for the conclusion that half or more of marriages end in divorce. The situation is bad, but not that bad. As was pointed out in a *Houston Chronicle* editorial replying to this charge: "98% of couples who live together are married. The U. S. has the highest divorce rate in the world, but 994.7 of every thousand do NOT get divorced!" (Oct. 23, 1981).

In other parts of the world, there are different problems, depending on the historical background of the country in religion and society. But there have been recent changes everywhere.

DIVORCES IN THE CHURCH

The church cannot ignore the changes in the community, since the church itself is affected. Most pastors find it difficult to preach strongly against divorce because of the number of divorced persons in the congregation. Those of us who are older know what a great change this is from the past.

We now have to decide what is the best way to combat divorce in the church. Maybe the best way is to put the emphasis where Jesus put it—on the plan of God for marriage to last for life.

DIVORCES IN THE MINISTRY

The most serious problem the church has at this point is the sad fact of divorced ministers. When the pastor of a church goes through a divorce, it makes problems for the congregation. Some of the people may take his side, and some hers, thus dividing the church. And just as a divorce in a family affects all the members of both his and her families, so the divorce of a pastor affects all the members of the congregation. If the pastor wants to go on as pastor of the congregation, the problems are compounded. If the pastor quickly remarries, the problems are multiplied.

It is not enough for the pastor to consider that he or she had a *legal* right to get the divorce. Even if the pastor is the one against whom the divorce action was taken, problems are still there. For one thing, the congregation can never know all the facts. Some of those facts are too private to be aired. For another, what the people do not know, they will guess at, and too often at the expense of the pastor's character.

Besides the effect on the congregation, there is the whole community to consider.

The pastor may know in the heart that he or she is innocent of sin. The pastor may even recognize and admit to God personal failure in the marriage. But what can the church and the community know of that? In the whole community there will be those who are for the pastor and those who are against. There are some who may not care much either way, but they know that the pastor went through a divorce. Their perception of the church and of the pastor is colored by their knowledge of that fact. The pastor can never again have just the same influence in the church and in the community as if the divorce had not taken place.

The responsible pastor will consider far more than his or her own blamelessness and will recognize that a pastor is responsible to the congregation and to the community in which it is located. Paul said that if eating meat would cause a brother to stumble, he would eat no more meat for the rest of his life. In the same way, the pastor who sees that his or her marriage is falling apart should immediately seek professional help. If the pastor's marriage is not strong, how can the pastor help others to build strong marriages?

It is not enough for the pastor who is divorcing or being divorced to have the support of some or most of the congregation. Their moral support may be good and helpful, but the pastor must consider the eventual effect on the whole work of the church.

3

MARRIAGE IN THE BIBLE

ANCIENT NEAR EASTERN BACKGROUND

It is always helpful for us, in studying the Old Testament, to consider what archeologists have learned about the customs and manners of people in those times. By studying what has been learned about the countries around the Israelites, we learn much about their own customs and the cultures which influenced them.

There is almost nothing in the Bible about marriage ceremonies. But it is likely that by the time of Christ the ceremonies centered around the betrothal and the marriage feast. Since the Bible says so little, most of what we know is guessed at by considering modern Arabic customs. But this is somewhat like guessing at marriage customs in the Middle Ages by considering Modern English practice.

The basic concept behind the ceremonies is that of the new family and its relationship with the relatives of both. The marriage is contracted publicly before the relatives. Yet we must understand that it was a religious, not secular, ceremony since the Bible made no distinction between the two. Every act was religious, and God controlled and judged all of life.

Betrothal was much more binding and formal than an engagement today. It could only be broken by a divorce, as among the Arabs and Syrians even today. This is why Matthew says that Joseph was about to divorce Mary, although it was clear that they were betrothed and had not yet consummated the marriage.

THE BIBLICAL TEACHING

One of the most basic and important facts about marriage which we learn from the Bible is that marriage is a divine institution. God instituted it (Gen. 2:18, 24), and we are told about it in the story of creation. This fact emphasizes the plan of God for mankind to build families and fill the earth.

The word for husband is *ish,* meaning "man" and the word for wife (also translated "marriage") is *ishshah.* To some, this indicates the naturalness with which the Old Testament expects men and women to marry. Even though the two words are not etymologically related, the play on words emphasizes the close relationship which God planned between husband and wife in marriage.

MARRIAGE IS PLEASING TO GOD

Some Christians have thought of marriage

as somehow second best and have felt that it would be more godly to remain single. They have had a vague feeling that sex is not truly Christian, but only something to be tolerated. However, there is no hint in the Bible that marriage is less than best for human beings.

Marriage is clear in the Old Testament that God commended marriage (Prov. 18:22). Further, the Old Testament writers give many indications that marriage is the normal state of human beings (Jdg. 11:37; Ps. 78:63; Isa. 4:1). And the New Testament does the same (1 Cor. 7:2; 1 Tim. 5:14; Eph. 5:31). And in Hebrews 13:4, we find the explicit statement that marriage is honorable.

It is so often the symbol of God and his people. The wife is to her husband what the church is to Christ. Nothing higher can be said about marriage than this.

This was denied by many early Christian fathers who taught that celibacy was more spiritual than marriage. Some of these were Ignatius, Justin Martyr, Tatian, Origen, Tertullian, Jerome, and even Augustine.

These individuals were influenced by the gnostic Greek philosophy which said that matter was contaminating to the spiritual soul and that one must purify the soul with asceticism. Only in this way could one rise above the lower physical nature. This attitude was based on the concept that the body is a prison for the spiritual soul, which longs to be set free to become part of God.

But the Reformation was a return to the scriptural teaching that the body was made by God and is pleasing to him. All Protestants denied the celibacy of the clergy. The Greek Orthodox Church had always denied celibacy, glorifying marriage.

MARRIAGE IS BOTH DIVINE AND CIVIL

Marriage is divine because the vows are made not only to each other but to God. If this is recognized, then it does not have to be a ceremony before a minister; the vows simply can be made before the gathered congregation, as is done among some Quakers. Yet Christians ought to emphasize the religious aspect.

Marriage today is also civil because of the social and civil relationships in our society. There are civil obligations which the state must recognize and enforce. The husband must support the wife, and the state can enforce this requirement. Marriage involves rights to property, and these rights are controlled by the state, not by the church. So marriage in our modern society is both religious and civil. So is divorce, for the same reason.

Since this is true, it is never enough for a Christian to prove that he or she has a legal right to divorce or remarry. That would mean that the action would satisfy the civil law, but the Christian must consider what would be pleasing to God. This point must be kept clear in our minds as we study the Scripture. A legal divorce is not necessarily pleasing to God.

GOD PLANNED MONOGAMY

It is clear from Genesis 2:24 that God planned for monogamy to be the form of marriage: one man and one woman. "For this reason a man will leave his father and mother and be united to his wife, and they will become one flesh." Lest we think that this is simply an Old Testament concept not applicable to Christians, we can note that Jesus quoted this verse as the norm for marriage (Matt. 19:3-6). Paul also quoted the verse for the same reason (Eph. 5:31).

We can see from this same verse also that God planned in the beginning for marriage to last for life. The two are to become one by their commitment to one another. This oneness is to last as long as they live. This is confirmed in the New Testament by Jesus (Matt. 19:3-6) and Paul (Rom. 7:2; 1 Cor. 7:39).

"ONE FLESH"

This oneness is emphasized by pointing out that they are "no more two, but one flesh." The concept of two becoming one indicates the way in which husband and wife are so intimately connected that they share all the experiences of life, both good and bad. This oneness of the marriage bond is often emphasized. The same idea is found in the concept of the wife as "helper." They are to help one another all the way through life. In all the experiences of life they are to help one another.

The two persons are not one in any metaphysical sense, but they are one in the sense that they have covenanted together to live together, work together, and share together as a team. As two horses become one team, or a group of persons becomes one company, so two persons, a man and a woman, become one in marriage.

This concept of oneness through covenant becomes important when we consider if, when, and how a marriage can be dissolved. The Bible does not say a marriage cannot be dissolved but that it should not be.

THE NATURE OF MARRIAGE

William F. Luck has a helpful discussion of two concepts of marriage which may be common, but unscriptural (1987, 223-237). First he shows that marriage is not essentially sexual in nature. That is, sexual intercourse is not equivalent to marriage. Two people can have intercourse without being thereby married, as can be seen by the laws in Exodus 22:16-17 and Deuteronomy 22:28-29. Marriage did not automatically follow. Note also the fact that Paul said that intercourse with a prostitute made them both one flesh. Yet they were not married and should not be. The truth is rather that marriage, with its serious covenant, is the only proper context for sexual intercourse.

Luck also points out the error of calling marriage a mystery. Usually this comes from a misunderstanding of Ephesians 5:32; Paul here did not call marriage a mystery but the relation of Christ to the church. And we need to remember that the Greek word *mysterion* does not mean something which cannot be understood, but rather something which would not be known if it were not revealed. Understanding the error of this concept will help us to avoid a wrong emphasis on the idea of "one flesh."

Marriage is not a mystical union of souls into one. If this were true, marriage would continue into eternity. But Jesus said clearly that there is no marriage in heaven, and so marriage is an institution made only for this life. Marriage does not result in an eternal union of souls, but is rather a covenant oneness of purpose and should result in the sharing of all things. This kind of oneness is not automatic; it comes from a united, strong effort to become more and more one.

We must understand also that an even worse misinterpretation of Ephesians 5:32 was the Roman Catholic view of marriage as a sacrament. This was built on the Vulgate use of the Latin word *sacramentum* as a translation of the Greek *mysterion*.

This is the concept which had caused the Roman Catholics to deny the possibility of divorce. Instead, they built up a list of reasons for annulment of marriages, thus avoiding "divorce." Erasmus argued against this artificial substitution of annulment for divorce in his exegesis of the divorce passages in the New Testament.

THE BIBLE IS NOT MISOGYNIST!

It is true that the Bible grew out of and was written in a culture of male dominatim. But it looks ahead and transcends its culture in this way as it also does in the worship of idols. By New Testament times it has made a major change in the roles of men and women. Jesus did not make specific statements about the wickedness of mistreating women any more than he did about slavery. In the matter of slavery, which was common in Jesus' time, Jesus did not fight it directly; instead he taught principles which eventually ended it. Now we can look back and see that Jesus' concern for the value of the individual leaves no room for one person to own another. It is the same with the treatment of women.

JESUS AND WOMEN

Jesus did not pay much attention to the usual human categorizing of people. Take, for example, the shepherds. Shepherds were looked down upon by the priests and Pharisees because they could not leave their sheep for the many temple or synagogue services and rituals. So the Pharisees called all of them sinners and avoided them. But when Jesus was born, it was not in the temple that the angels brought the message, but to the shepherds in their lonely vigil in the fields.

Jesus treated women with the same respect he showed to men, making no difference between them. No Jewish rabbi in the time of Christ would condescend to discuss theology with a woman or a group of women. But Jesus initiated such a discussion, not only with a woman, but with a woman of the despised Samaritans (John 4). He then used her as a missionary-evangelist in her hometown. When his disciples saw him in a serious discussion of theology with a woman, they were astonished. And they were even more astonished that it was a Samaritan woman. To Jesus, she was only another needy person.

Jesus interrupted an errand of mercy for a ruler of the synagogue to talk with a woman who needed help. She had suffered for twelve years from an affliction which had kept her from being permitted in the synagogue or being touched by others (Matt. 9:20-22; cf. Lev. 15:25). He never treated any woman as if she were inferior.

In Luke 10:38-42 Jesus said it was better for Mary to listen to Jesus' teaching than to be a busy hostess doing "women's" work. In Luke 15:8-10 he compared God to a woman! He used women in his parables (Matt. 13:33; 25:1; Luke 15:8; 18:1).

In John 8:1-11 he refused to condemn the adulterous woman *more than* the man, who was not brought to judgment (cf. Deut. 22:22-24).

In Matthew 18:20 the rabbis said no service was valid without *ten men*. Jesus made no distinction! Even two women could be sure of God's blessing.

Jesus had women followers early in his ministry (Luke 8:1-3). They helped provide support and hospitality and even followed him to the cross (Luke 23:49; Mark 15:40-41).

Jesus chose only men as his twelve disciples. But these are not our pattern for choosing preachers. Do we have to have one Judas to every eleven preachers? He had many women among his other disciples.

When Jesus died, one of his last thoughts was of a woman, Mary his mother, and of her future. When he rose from the dead he first appeared to a woman and sent her to give a message to the eleven.

MARRIAGE IS FOR THIS LIFE ONLY

God planned marriage for this life only. We learn this from the reply of Jesus to those who asked a complicated question about marriage (Matt. 22:30; Mark. 12:25; Luke 20:35-36). A widow married six more husbands, each of whom died, and finally she died. They asked, "Now then, at the resurrection, whose wife will she be of the seven, since all of them were married to her?" Jesus made it clear that there will be no marriage in heaven, where we will be like angels in this respect. We will not return to a pre-pubertal state, but we will have transcended sex. We shall have relationships with one another which far transcend that of husband and wife. The fact that we cannot imagine what such a state could be does not in any way argue against the possibility. We take the word of Christ for that.

POLYGAMY IN THE BIBLE

In the Old Testament, before the time of the Babylonian Exile, kings and leaders, and sometimes common people, had more than one wife. Prominent persons such as Abraham, David, and Solomon had many wives. Although this is not found among God's people after the Exile, nor in the New Testament, this makes a problem for Christians. How shall we think of those who practiced polygamy yet seemed to be blessed by God?

The difference between polygamy and adultery was that each wife was legally married, with mutual commitment to each other. It was not a casual arrangement.

Yet polygamy was neither God's plan nor God's ideal for man. God made one wife for Adam and insisted that this was the proper way. God tolerated polygamy for the time being "because of the hardness of their hearts" but at the same time let men and women suffer on account of forsaking the ideal. So the Bible records the jealousy, fighting, and sorrows which accompanied this deviation from God's will. The story of Solomon tells of the way his polygamy led to the downfall of his kingdom (1 Kings 11). Nowhere is it commanded. Jesus strongly approved only one man and one woman for life!

4

THE UNMARRIED

There are three classes of single Christians who need to know what the Bible says about their condition: those who have never been married, which includes young men and women; the widowed; and the divorced. They all have some of the same problems, though certain problems may be more acute in those in their teen years. We will deal with some of these.

What does the Bible have to say to youth before they are married? They have problems with sexual urges which are most difficult, and often they feel they have no one who can help them. Does the Bible do any more than condemn them for their mistakes and blunders? Is the Bible too perfectionistic to be of any practical help? Is sexual desire sinful?

SEX IS GOOD

The Bible does have some important things to say to the young and single, some of which are most helpful. It is too bad that the church is not able to get the message across to all youth as soon as they need it.

The first thing we should learn in the Bible about sex is that God instituted it. In the story of creation we are told that "God created man in his own image, in the image of God he created him; male and female he created them. God blessed them and said to them, 'Be fruitful and increase in number' " (Gen. 1:27-28a).

This was before human beings had sinned. Sex is not in any way a part of the fall of mankind. It was after this that God said of all he had created that "it was very good" (Gen. 1:31). This makes it clear that God considered the sexual nature of mankind to be very good! Startling as it may seem to some who have been taught otherwise, this is what the Bible says. Sex is part of the plan of God for human beings, as well as for the animals.

Sex is good, just as the appetite for food or the love of beauty is good. But this is not to say that sexual appetite is to be satisfied any time and any place. This would make no more sense than to seek to eat everything which looks appetizing or to acquire everything which appears beautiful. There are those who have said that sex is as natural as eating, and so we ought not to be afraid or ashamed of indulging in sex any time we please. This may be true of dogs, but we are not dogs. We are human beings, with a sense of propriety which animals do not have. We have minds which put us on a different level from the merely physical.

Look at the appetite for food. No matter how hungry we are, we recognize that eating is more than the satisfaction of hunger. We find that eating is best done when certain formalities are observed. We put the food on a table and seek to make the table attractive. We sit down at the table, pray, courteously help others get the food they want, and eat with some concern for "manners." In this way, food is not merely eaten to satisfy our hunger, but we use the time and the place for fellowship with one another. This is not the only way to eat, and there are situations in which these formalities are impossible, but we find that this is the most satisfactory way. Observance of formalities in eating even helps the digestion! And it certainly makes eating more pleasant.

We do not eat everything we want, if we care about our own bodies. And we certainly do not take food which belongs to others. We do not eat all the time. Our health is best if we have regular times and places for eating and if we carefully regulate the amount and nature of the food we eat. We know that what and how we eat can extend our life or shorten it. So we learn to exercise care in our eating.

Some of this is true also of our sexual appetite, though there are differences. Food is essential if we are to stay alive, but sex is not. We can live a long, healthy life with no sexual intercourse at all. Marriage is not necessary to health and happiness. This means that we must not treat the two alike.

SEX IN MARRIAGE IS GOOD

If we look again at the context of the creation statement about man and woman, we see that God planned not merely for sex but for life-long marriage: "For this reason a man will leave his father and mother and be united to his wife, and they will become one flesh" (Gen. 2:24). Jesus later quoted this verse as proof of God's intention for marriage to be for life (Matt. 19:4-5). So marriage is what God planned for human beings for the purpose of multiplying and perpetuating their numbers.

Note that the New Testament explicitly states that marriage is honorable: "Marriage should be honored by all, and the marriage bed kept pure, for God will judge the adulterer and all the sexually immoral" (Heb. 13:4). This means that there is nothing spiritually or morally wrong with marriage, though it does not mean that being unmarried is dishonorable. Paul makes it clear that one should be content with either alternative and be concerned only with doing the will of God (1 Cor. 7:17).

FORNICATION IS PROHIBITED

The same passage in Hebrews which tells that marriage is honorable tells us that God will judge those who are sexually immoral. Fornication and adultery—sex outside of marriage—are forbidden here and elsewhere in the Bible. This is true in both the Old and New Testaments, as can be seen by reading a few passages: Matthew 15:19; Acts 15:20, 29; 21:25; 1 Corinthians 6:13, 18; 10:8; Galatians 5:19.

This means that sex outside of marriage is wrong, harmful, and sinful. It is not simply that God wrote it down on the sinful side of the ledger. It is sinful because it is wrong and harmful to all concerned. It is sinful because it is not the way God planned for human beings to live. God made sexual attraction as one of the strongest of human emotions so that it would draw us together and cause us to overcome obstacles in order to make a life-long commitment to one another. This commitment is the heart of marriage. This is the plan of God.

LIVING TOGETHER UNMARRIED IS WRONG

The fact that sex outside of marriage is wrong means that the recent increase of couples living together without marriage is sinful. They say the only difference between that and marriage is a piece of paper, but that is not true. The difference is in the commitment to one another for life, which is made in marriage. And this is a great difference. Many of those who practice this living together are simply afraid to make a commitment. Some of them are afraid because their own parents made a failure of marriage. Others have a low self-image so that they are afraid no one will ever love them enough for marriage. Still others feel unloved and are seeking for any crumb of caring that will substitute for the love they need. But whatever the reasons, this is not the solution.

CAN THE SINGLE BE PURE?

As almost every young person knows, it is not easy to keep a pure mind and heart in a world like this. It is not only that there are attractive persons around. There are also all the temptations to lust.

We live in a sex oriented world. It is much like living in ancient Corinth, where there were temple prostitutes, and to be with them was considered a part of the religion. America is not all that different: consider the talk of free sex on television, pornographic literature everywhere, and novels, magazines, and movies which trumpet the wonders of freedom in sexual encounters. All of this makes it difficult for the sincere Christian who wants to keep a pure heart. Is it possible to have a pure heart in a world like this?

Jesus began his Sermon on the Mount with blessings upon the people who please God and said, "Blessed are the pure in heart, for they will see God" (Matt. 5:8). A few verses later he said, "But I tell you that anyone who looks at a woman lustfully has already committed adultery with her in his heart" (v. 28). This verse has caused anguish to many a young Christian man. It seems to them to condemn all sexual desire, and they find it impossible to quench that desire completely. So they feel condemned. Is the Bible unrealistic?

Several things need to be said about this verse from Jesus. First, Jesus did not say that seeing beauty in a woman was sin, nor that admiring beauty is sinful. He was pointing out, as he had already done with other sins, that the sin does not begin with an unlawful act. Sin begins in the heart, and what is in the heart begins in the mind. Second, the Greek tense he uses for the word *look* implies duration: to "gaze at" or to "keep on looking."

Third, he added the word *lustfully*. Some scholars feel that the Greek expression could be translated "for the purpose of lusting after." Fourth, he said "in his heart." It is not merely that the thought of adultery has entered the mind, but because of the continued meditating on the desire, the thought of adultery has entered into the heart and is sin. The old proverb goes: "You can't keep the birds from flying over your head, but you can keep them from building a nest in your hair." So it is with thoughts. You cannot prevent thoughts and impulses from entering your mind, but you can keep them from finding a home there and sinking into your heart and life.

HOW TO KEEP PURE

Keeping a pure heart as a single is not easy, but it can be done. We can gain some help from Ephesians 5:1-4:

Be imitators of God, therefore, as dearly loved children and live a life of love, just as Christ loved us and gave himself up for us as a fragrant offering and sacrifice to God. But among you there must not be even a hint of sexual immorality, or of any kind of impurity, or of greed, because these are improper for God's holy people. Nor should there be obscenity, foolish talk or coarse joking, which are out of place, but rather thanksgiving.

Now note that in the previous chapter in Ephesians (4:17), Paul had said that we must not live like the ungodly people around us. We should instead live lives of love for God and love for one another. But in this kind of world we need to know that love is not the lust of which most people speak and think. Godly love is quite different from the kind of thing most people call love. Godly love is the kind of self-sacrificing love which God had for us in Jesus Christ, who gave up his own life on the cross to save us from sin. This kind of love will not tolerate sexual immorality or impure talk about it. Sexual love must not be spoken of with impurity of language. We must not joke about sex or speak foolishly, with obscenity or coarse joking, "which are out of place" and "are improper for God's holy people."

Paul points out at the end of this passage that the Christian attitude toward sexual love begins with thanksgiving to God for giving it to us. If we once come to the point of giving thanks to God for our libido, then we can dedicate our whole self to God, including this aspect of self which seems so hard to control. This is the beginning of true victory.

God does not require of us what he cannot help us to do by his grace. When God said for us to keep our hearts pure, he meant that he would make this possible by the help of his Holy Spirit.

5

MUTUAL RESPONSIBILITIES

MUTUAL LOVE AND SUBMISSION

We see in the Bible that God plans for the two to become one through love for one another and through mutual submission (Eph. 5:21-25; Titus 2:3-5). This submission is often said to be one-sided. The wife must submit to the husband all the time and in everything. But in Ephesians 5:21, Paul first said, "Submit to *one another* out of reverence for Christ" (italics added). Only after that did he command the wife to submit to her husband. And in the paragraphs which follow, he said much more about the husband's love for his wife than about her submission to him. It is only the self-giving love of the husband for his wife which makes it fitting for her to submit to him. Further, the command of mutual submission is the overall rule. Each must submit to the other.

If two people are to be one in more than words, then there must be mutual love, respect, and submission in the way they relate to one another. Verse 22 has no verb in the best Greek texts. The paragraph division here is by a later editor. So Paul was saying: "Submit yourselves to one another, wives to your own husbands as to the Lord."

Just as children are to obey their parents "in the Lord," so husbands and wives are to be submissive in attitude toward one another so as to please the Lord. Mutual submission has nothing to do with superiority or inferiority, but rather with the humble Christian attitude which can please God and hold the marriage together. Only mutual submission is compatible with the subsequent commands to the husbands to love their wives with the kind of love with which Christ loved the church. Godly love expresses itself in mutual submission.

RESPONSIBILITIES OF HUSBANDS TO THEIR WIVES

It is interesting and helpful to note that the Bible describes some of the ways in which husbands and wives ought to act toward one another. Full attention to them will make for better and more lasting marriages.

We begin with the responsibilities of husbands.

1. Love their wives. In Ephesians 5:25, Paul not only says that husbands should love their wives, but that it ought to be done with the same kind of love with which Christ loved the church. Jesus died for the sake of the church. The husband should then love his

wife enough to give his own life, if necessary, for the sake of his wife! He says further that "husbands ought to love their wives as their own bodies" (v. 28). He adds in verse 33 that "each one of you also must love his wife as he loves himself." (Compare also Col. 3:19 and Gen. 2:23.)

2. Be faithful to them. The whole point of marriage is for the man and the woman to be faithful to each other. But this is made explicit in Malachi 2:14-15, which concludes with the admonition: "So guard yourself in your spirit, and do not break faith with the wife of your youth." See also Hebrews 13:4.

Faithfulness is not merely refraining from certain actions. As Jesus emphasized in the Sermon on the Mount, sin begins with the thoughts and attitudes of the heart. It is not only murder which is sin, but anger toward the other person (Matt. 5:21-22). It is not only adultery which is wrong, but lust for another woman. And that begins with simple desire which is dwelt upon (Matt. 5:27-28). So faithfulness requires that a man cultivate love for his own wife and fix his thoughts only on her. In this way his love for his own wife can grow so as to blot out any desire for others which could creep in. Such love for his wife can help the marriage last for life.

Faithfulness is also cultivated by determination to make the marriage work and last. This determination is part of the commitment which ought to be a part of every marriage from the outset. Without it, no marriage has much of a chance.

3. Comfort them. In 1 Samuel 1:8 we read of the way in which Hannah's husband, El-kanah, sought to comfort her in her grief at not having children. Giving comfort in a time of sorrow or trouble is one of the ways in which true love can be shown. In such a time, the husband has a chance to show just how much love he does have for his wife. To give true comfort then requires self-giving love, the kind of love Christ had for the church. This kind of love can reveal itself not merely in giving up one's physical life for the other, but in giving of one's time, energy, and strength to the other when she needs it.

4. Stay with them for life. In Matthew 19:4-6 Jesus made it clear that it is the plan of God for a husband to forsake all others and stay with his wife for all of life — "till death do us part." He never said it would be easy but that it was the right thing to do.

In spite of the wording in the traditional marriage vows about "for better or worse; in sickness and in health . . ." most young couples have such stars in their eyes that they cannot even imagine some of the things which can happen to make it hard to stay together for life. But troubles do come to most, and life together does sometimes seem impossible. At such times, what is needed is a conscious commitment to stay together no matter what happens or how hard it gets.

In 1 Corinthians 7:12 Paul discussed one of the circumstances in Corinth which made it hard for some marriages to last. In that verse he spoke of the fact that some married men had been converted from the worship of idols, but their wives were not Christian. We can imagine the problems which arose when the wife went to the pagan temple to worship and then brought home meat which had been dedicated to an idol and served it to her Christian husband. Paul dealt specifically with this aspect of the problem in 1 Corinthians 8.

And there were other problems which became severe when the Christian husband refused to participate with his wife in some of her activities because of his new Christian standards. But Paul insisted that if the wife is ready to stay with him, he should not break up the marriage because of these serious problems. The marriage vows were to be kept for life.

RESPONSIBILITIES OF WIVES TO THEIR HUSBANDS

Just as the Bible instructs us regarding the responsibilities of husbands for their wives, so it gives some indications of what wives should do for their husbands. It becomes clear that each has a part to play in marriage and that neither can do the whole job alone. Some have called marriage a "fifty-fifty" compact, so that each gives half. But that will not work. Marriage is a commitment where each person gives all he or she has to make it good. Each must share l00 percent of his or her strength, love, and ability, never checking to see if the other is doing enough.

So we look now at the responsibilities of the wives:

1. Love their husbands. Paul pointed out that it was the responsibility of the older women to teach the younger women to "love their husbands and children" (Titus 2:4). In all of these commands for husbands and wives to love each other, we must remind ourselves that "love" in the Bible means so much more than romantic emotions. In fact, Christian love is not an emotion but a way of living and acting. Christian love is not an emotion which controls the person but it is a conscious giving of oneself to the other. This will create plenty of emotion, but the giving of self, not the emotion, is real love.

So the wife should love her husband, just as the husband should love the wife. Since this love is a way of acting, it is under the control of the wife. She can decide to give him her love and train herself to do this always. In this she is no different from him.

2. Respect their husbands. Paul concludes Ephesians 5:33 by saying that "the wife must respect her husband." He uses here the same Greek word as is used in Leviticus 19:3 (LXX) of respect for parents. It is the same respect which is due to anyone having authority, position, or responsibility. We are to respect the office, or the responsibility, whether we can respect the person or not. The child should respect the parents just because they

are parents. By being parents, they have responsibility for the children, whether they are worthy parents or not.

Of course, this respect is mutual, just as submission is to be mutual. Each must respect the other. In Ephesians 5:33, Paul began the sentence with the repeated command for the husband to love his wife, which includes respect for her. Each must respect the other and show proper regard for the responsibilities and needs of the other. Only in this way can they cooperate to make the marriage a good one.

But what if the husband is not worthy of respect? What is the Christian wife to do then? We have then the same situation as the child who has an unworthy father. He cannot obey wicked commands of the father, but as long as he is in that home, he must respect the fact that his father is his parent. He is to treat his father respectfully, even when he cannot respect his father's way of living. It is the same with the wife.

If the wickedness of the husband is such that it makes it impossible any longer for her to treat him respectfully, then she is in a difficult situation and must decide what can be done about that sick marriage. But the principle is true that they cannot live together as a family without showing proper respect for one another.

3. Be faithful to them. Just as the husband is commanded to be faithful to his own wife, so the wife is commanded to be faithful to

her own husband (1 Cor. 7:2-5, 10). This takes the same kind of commitment and work which is required for the man to be faithful. Just as the husband must work at growing his love for his wife, so the wife must work at making her love for her husband grow. She must not be gazing longingly at other men but concentrate on her faithfulness to her own husband.

4. Remain with them for life. Marriage is for life, as both the husband and wife must understand (Rom. 7:2-3; 1 Cor. 7:39). The wife must then commit herself to living with her husband as long as they both shall live and concentrate her efforts on doing all that will make this possible. The commitment at the beginning is the important factor. If she feels from the beginning that she will try him out, and if she does not like him she will leave him, then the marriage is not likely to last very long. But if she goes into the marriage determined to make it last as long as she lives, then she can do it.

All that is said of the faithfulness of the husband applies to the wife as well. The two must each contribute his or her best to the marriage.

6

DIVORCE IN THE OLD TESTAMENT

The basic Old Testament passage on divorce is Deuteronomy 24:1-4. But even this does not discuss divorce in general but gives only a special case. There is no general law in the whole Bible making divorce an accepted procedure. This passage simply places certain controls on the divorce procedure, at least in this particular case. We should look at the whole passage:

If a man marries a woman who becomes displeasing to him because he finds something indecent about her, and he writes her a certificate of divorce, gives it to her and sends her from his house, and if after she leaves his house she becomes the wife of another man, and her second husband dislikes her and writes her a certificate of divorce, gives it to her and sends her from his house, or if he dies, then her first husband, who divorced her, is not allowed to marry her again after she has been defiled. That would be detestable in the eyes of the Lord. Do not bring sin upon the land the Lord your God is giving you as an inheritance (Deut. 24:1-4, NIV).

The older versions divide this into three sentences and makes it sound like a law regulating divorce. However, it is not really a law of divorce but pertains to the concept of remarrying another wife and then divorcing that one and remarrying the first wife. Judging from Jesus' remarks about this passage, it cannot be interpreted as a divine sanction of divorce. The fact is that no Scripture puts God's approval on divorce, though this passage tolerates it and thus regulates it.

Divorce is never mandatory. The lawyers who came to Jesus in Matthew 19 sought to imply that Moses commanded divorce, but Jesus quietly corrected them, stating that Moses only permitted it under certain circumstances because of their hardness of heart. And he pointed out that in such a case, the divorce was carefully controlled by the rules laid down here.

It is not known what was the "unseemly thing" which justified divorce. The rabbis in the time of Christ differed strongly on its identity. But more on this later.

Actually, the laws regulating divorce are for the benefit of the wife. They make it harder for the man to get the divorce than it was in the nations around Israel.

Since divorce was denied to some (Deut.

22:13-21) there had to be some kind of trial to make sure that it was legal and at which there would be some persuasion against the divorce. Then three requirements had to be met: (1) A scribe had to write up the divorce in proper legal form. (2) The decree of divorce must be placed in the hand of the wife so that she would have legal proof. (3) She had to leave his house.

The "bill of divorcement" (Hebrew *sepher kerithuth*) was for the sake of the wife who might otherwise be left destitute, without even the right to marry another man and be a significant part of the community.

The usual form of such a decree is given by W. W. Davies (1929 2:864):

> On the _____ day of the week _____ in the month _____ in the year _____ from the beginning of the world, according to the common computation in the province of _____ I _____ the son of _____ by whatever name I may be known, of the town of _____ with entire consent of mind, and without any constraint, have divorced, dismissed and expelled thee _____ daughter of _____ by whatever name thou art called, of the town _____ who has been my wife hitherto; But now I have dismissed thee _____ the daughter of _____ by whatever name thou art called, of the town of _____ so as to be free at thy own disposal, to marry whomsoever thou

pleasest, without hindrance from anyone, from this day for ever. Thou art therefore free for anyone who would marry thee. Let this be thy bill of divorce from me, a writing of separation and expulsion, according to the law of Moses and Israel.

_____ the son of _____, witness
_____ the son of _____, witness

One further enlightening point is that according to the Talmud, the woman was to receive at the divorce her original dowry plus an equal amount from her husband. This means that she left the marriage with twice the money, property, and lands that she brought to it. She could not be left without financial protection!

So we see that the law gives the wife certain rights: (1) The right to have some financial support. (2) The right to remarry. (3) The right to be separated from a husband who does not want her. (4) The right to have a legal divorce with her rights protected. He could not merely desert her.

Since the husband did not have to accuse the wife of adultery to be divorced, she was not forced to prove her innocence in order for the divorce to be granted.

We see the uniqueness of the Old Testament when we compare it with the laws of marriage and divorce in the countries of the ancient Near East. Only the Bible has such a high view of the marriage bond and such concern for the rights of the wife in the event of separation.

LEGITIMATE REASONS FOR DIVORCE

The Jewish Talmud devotes a section on the concept of divorce, and it is here that we find the conclusions of the two schools of thought—Shammai and Hillel. Rabbi Shammai felt that divorce was legitimate only on the ground of adultery.

The fact is that though there has been much discussion by the greatest of scholars over the meaning of "shameful thing" (Hebrew, 'erweth dabar), there is no agreement as to what it means. We know meanings of each of the two words, but not what this Hebrew idiom meant in this connection.

John Murray ("Divorce," Dictionary of Theology, Grand Rapids: Baker, 1960), is sure that this could not be adultery, since death was the penalty for that (Lev. 20:10; Deut. 22:22-27). He also believes it could not be suspected adultery, since that was to be tested by trial (cf. Num. 5:11-31). However, one wonders how often these trials were practiced, if ever. And we know that stoning was seldom done by the Jews in Roman times, as it could bring trouble from the Romans.

In Brown-Driver-Briggs' book, A Hebrew and English Lexicon of the Old Testament (New York: Harper and Sons, 1907), it is suggested that it "probably" means "indecency, improper behavior." Probably it is best to translate it by "sexual immorality," since it includes all kinds of unfaithfulness and sexual sins.

Rabbi Hillel (Babylonian Talmud, "Gittin," ix, 10) and his followers, on the other hand, felt that this passage permitted divorce for any reason whatever, for example, if she burned his food, if she talked too loudly, or if he found a prettier woman. They emphasized the words "if then she finds no favor in his eyes."

Some scholars feel that the questioners of Jesus were trying to get him to take sides with either Hillel or Shammai. They could then say either that he was too lax or too strict, and thus cause him to lose some following. But as we shall see later, this is too simple a solution.

However some of the questions about the passage may be resolved, it is clear that we can learn something of the message of Moses about marriage. Edward Dobson (1989, 40) suggests the following principles may be summarized from the law of Moses on divorce:

1. God instituted marriage, but man invented divorce.
2. Divorce required legal steps and a document.
3. Remarriage was permitted.
4. Divorce provided for the rights of the wife.
5. God commands permanence in marriage.

So we must be clear about the message of the Old Testament. Though divorce was permitted in certain circumstances, it was never the full will of God. As Jesus pointed out, it was merely tolerated because of the hard-heartedness of people. But it was carefully regulated and looked upon as a failure of the marriage. It was practiced in Old Testament times, as we can see from the laws against a priest marrying any divorcee (Lev. 21:7, 14). We also see special rules about divorced persons (Lev. 22:13; Num. 30:9; Deut. 22:13-29). But it was considered less than the best. God made marriage and intended it to last for all of life. Divorce, then, is a failure to fulfill God's will. Thus God says, "I hate divorce" (Mal. 2:16).

7

DIVORCE IN THE GOSPELS

Matthew 5:31-32

It is wise to begin with the study of the words of Jesus. And it is good to begin with his first great sermon in which he introduced the Kingdom of God and described the people who make it up.

He emphasized first his support of the Old Testament. But he showed that he could not agree with the common interpretations of the Old Testament, as they were evasions of the real meaning. So he insisted that members of the Kingdom must have a righteousness which exceeds that of the Pharisees and lawyers of the day.

Jesus then gave six illustrations of shallow interpretations of the Old Testament and showed how we must interpret these passages. He considered the commands against murder, adultery, divorce, oaths, revenge, and love for others. In each case he insisted that we must consider sin as beginning in the heart, and so the commands are to be more strictly applied to attitudes, not just to outward actions.

After discussing adultery, Jesus turned to the idea of divorce: "It has been said, 'Anyone who divorces his wife must give her a certificate of divorce.' But I tell you that anyone who divorces his wife, except for marital unfaithfulness, causes her to become an adulteress, and anyone who marries the divorced woman commits adultery" (Matt. 5:31-32).

Jesus is referring to the command in Deuteronomy 24:1 that a man who divorces his wife must not be like the heathen nations who had a low view of marriage. Marriage is planned by God to last for life. It is to be marked by faithfulness to one another for as long as they both shall live. Divorce is not part of the plan of God. But if a man does decide to get rid of his wife, he must do it properly. He must not send her away with nothing, as some of the heathen did, but must give her a certificate of divorce, which involved a legal transaction.

THE PURPOSE OF JESUS

Look at what Jesus was seeking to do in this part of the Sermon on the Mount. He was not seeking to lay down a new set of laws to supersede the Mosaic Law. He was not saying that the Old Testament was too soft and now he would be more strict in his rules. He did not come to destroy the law and the prophets (Matt. 5:17). It was his purpose instead to set down some basic principles which can guide us more surely than laws to do God's will.

Jesus told Peter not to forgive seven times, but seventy times seven in one day! He was not laying down a strict rule so that after 490 times one could then take revenge on the sinner or at least give up on him. Jesus was laying down a principle that the Christian must be a forgiving person even toward the sinner who keeps on sinning. Jesus emphasized his principles by overstating them by means of hyperbole and other ways.

WHAT JESUS SAID

We shall assume in the following discussion that Jesus said the words "except for adultery." This is not assumed by all New Testament scholars. The words are not found in Mark or Luke, but only in Matthew, where it occurs twice. Some have therefore suggested that Matthew included the words in order to soften the statement of Jesus or that, in what amounts to the same thing, the church decided that these words should be included.

Stephen S. Smalley has a helpful discussion of this point. He makes the point that even if the words were added by Matthew, it was not done to weaken the statement of Jesus but to emphasize it.

Matthew may be making explicit what was assumed by Jesus and the other evangelists, that divorce was made necessary by Jewish law when sexual irregularity was discovered among partners before or after marriage. Betrothed couples could separate when unfaithfulness was suspected, as in the case of Joseph and Mary (Matt. 1:19); and strict Hebrews insisted on divorce when marriage within the forbidden degrees of kinship was uncovered. In any case Matthew is reporting and upholding the principle laid down by Jesus, that marriage is a God-given ordinance within creation, and therefore to be regarded as hallowed . . . In no case may we claim that Matthew's redaction weakens the authority of the teaching he preserves, or departs from the mind of Christ (1977, 190).

It must be remembered that Matthew was writing to Jews who knew the Old Testament as the Word of God. Mark and Luke were both writing to Gentiles, who lived only under the Roman law. So the inclusion of the "exceptive clause" would mean something different to the two groups. The fact that Matthew included it should make the Jews feel even more guilty for the way they had sought to misuse the text in Deuteronomy. The others omitted it since it did not have the same relevance to the Greeks and Romans to whom they were writing.

When Jesus said that divorce hurts, and implied that the only possible excuse for it was sexual immorality, he was not saying that it was mandatory in the case of adultery or other sexual immorality. He did not say that everything short of the overt act of adultery was all right. He did not mean that one should hire a detective to see if the act was committed so one could have a divorce with impunity. He was not laying down a strict law by which to decide on divorce.

MARRIAGE IS FOR LIFE

He was saying instead that marriage is for life and that one must not destroy what God has made to last. He was stressing the importance of marriage and the importance of doing all in one's power to keep the marriage vow for all of life. That is the basic principle he espoused. Jesus did not work out the details of the day-by-day solutions to the problems of marriage and divorce. He left that for us to do. He knew that we live in an imperfect world, but he stressed the ideal. He stressed the original plan of God for lifelong marriage. We dare not do less.

Jesus did not say that marriage *could* not be broken; he said that it *should* not be broken. He clearly implied that it can be broken by sexual immorality, and divorce can be given on the basis of that immorality. But Jesus insisted that no Christian would commit such sins. He did not say that the Christian should rush to the divorce court if a partner committed such sins. Jesus did not discuss the differences of rabbinical opinions on the grounds for divorce, but he spoke instead of the divine plan for marriage to be permanent and for life.

"CAUSES HER TO COMMIT ADULTERY"

This expression, "causes her to commit adultery," has created considerable difficulty. How could the divorce force the woman to commit adultery? In seeking a solution, it has been suggested that the man simply puts her in a position where she might become an adulteress. But this does not make the statement very sensible.

It is more helpful to consider a better English translation of this unusual expression. The Greek verb here uses the passive form of the verb, which makes the divorced wife the object of some action. She is sinned against. She is the object of the action of the man who is divorcing her. She "suffers adultery." It is possible to get something of the idea of the Greek if we translate the statement this way: "Whoever divorces his wife except on the basis of infidelity makes her the object of his unfaithfulness." (Something similar is expressed in other ways by the commentaries of Ridderbos, Henderson, and Grosheide.)

Ronald J. Fowler has a good statement on this point:

Jesus clearly demonstrates that an innocent party (the wife) is made to appear guilty of action she did not commit. Therefore the man who follows the lax position of Hillel (divorce based on any reason), is guilty of sinning against the innocent wife and any who would marry her . . . . He makes both to appear to have committed an act (fornication) which in fact was not committed; he causes them to live under a cloud of sin which taints their character (Lewis 1978, 43-44).

Jesus was not interested in discussing the arguments of the two groups of Pharisees as to the grounds on which a husband could divorce his wife. He was concerned to point out the effect of the divorce on the innocent wife. And his emphasis was on the intention of God for marriage to be for all of life.

8

THE PHARISEES TEST JESUS

The passages in Matthew 5 and Luke 16 are different from those in Matthew 19 and Mark 10 in that the latter are in the context of a dispute with the Pharisees.
Matthew 19:3-9

Matthew 19:3-9

³Some Pharisees came to him to test him. They asked, "Is it lawful for a man to divorce his wife for any and every reason?"

⁴"Haven't you read," he replied, "that at the beginning the Creator 'made them male and female,' ⁵and said, 'For this reason a man will leave his father and mother and be united to his wife, and the two will become one flesh?' ⁶So they are no longer two, but one. Therefore what God has joined together, let man not separate."

⁷"Why then," they asked, "did Moses command that a man give his wife a certificate of divorce and send her away?"

⁸Jesus replied, "Moses permitted you to divorce your wives because your hearts were hard. But it was not this way from the beginning. ⁹I tell you that anyone who divorces his wife, except for marital unfaithfulness, and marries another woman commits adultery."

Mark 10:2-12

²Some Pharisees came and tested him by asking, "Is it lawful for a man to divorce his wife?"

³"What did Moses command you?" he replied.

⁴They said, "Moses permitted a man to write a certificate of divorce and send her away."

⁵"It was because your hearts were hard that Moses wrote you this law," Jesus replied. ⁶"But at the beginning of creation God 'made them male and female.' ⁷For this reason a man will leave his father and mother and be united to his wife, ⁸and the two will become one flesh.' So they are no longer two, but one. ⁹Therefore what God has joined together, let not man separate."

¹⁰When they were in the house again, the disciples asked Jesus about this. ¹¹He answered, "Anyone who divorces his wife and marries another woman commits adultery against her. ¹²And if she divorces her husband and marries another man, she commits adultery."

Luke 16:18

[18]"Anyone who divorces his wife and marries another woman commits adultery, and the man who marries a divorced woman commits adultery."

Notice two important points about this passage: First, the one exception (sexual immorality) underlines the wrongness of any other reason for divorce.

Second, Mark implies that the woman has a right to initiate divorce and that the same restriction applies to her (Mark 10:12).

Matthew alone says "except for adultery." Major questions have been raised: Did Jesus say these words, or were they added by Matthew or others? What is the meaning of the word *porneia*, translated "adultery?" Did Jesus forbid all divorce, or did he permit it for this one reason only—adulterous action by the wife? What were the Pharisees attempting to accomplish in so "testing" Jesus?

Is there any honest way to make a decision among the various contradictory answers given to these questions? Or must we conclude that the New Testament is so unclear at this point that we must simply choose the interpretation we like best?

VARIOUS INTERPRETATIONS

Instead of confusing the issue with outlines of the various interpretations at each point, we will briefly list some positions held by different scholars and evaluate them. It will not be necessary to list all the historic positions held through 2,000 years, but only the chief opinions held today by evangelical scholars.

At one end of the spectrum we have Heth, Laney, and Wenham, who insist that though divorce may be permitted in certain cases, remarriage is always wrong and divorce does not dissolve the marriage. Only death can end a marriage.

Writers such as Dobson, Stein, and Luck insist that divorce is failure but that we live in an imperfect world and must trust in God's forgiveness. Divorce ends a marriage, and so remarriage is to be permitted.

These opposing conclusions are supported by a variety of exegetical reasonings, which are at times difficult to follow. Let me express my conviction about these scholars at this point in my learning. My concluding pages will express what I have come to believe is the teaching of the Bible. Those pages were written in outline in 1962. The outline has not changed, though my support for those convictions has grown as I have continued to study. This may mean that I am reading into my study my own convictions, but I do not think so. I believe I have sought honestly and openmindedly for the truth. Let me also say that I would have come to different conclusions if I had written in the decade before 1960. In other words, I did once agree with the position of Heth and Wenham, even though they had not then written their books. I did change my mind through further study.

There are three points on which scholars disagree:

1. The exception clause in Matthew.
2. The meaning of *porneia* (adultery).
3. The validity of remarriage.

There are problems in agreeing with the reasoning of Heth and Wenham. Their reasoning and exegesis seems rather tortured, and though I have deeply appreciated most of the books by Wenham, it seems to me that in this study he is trying too hard to support his own opinions.

Heth and Wenham (1984) give a great deal of attention to what they call the "exception clause" ("except for marital unfaithfulness"), which is found only in Matthew 19:9. They base their understanding of the verse on the location of this clause in the sentence and on their interpretation of the teaching of the early church fathers. At this point we will only consider what they say about this clause.

Heth and Wenham give considerable space to proving that the order of words is important in Greek. All Greek scholars are aware of this fact and know that it does not change the meaning of a sentence as much as it does in a language such as English. But Heth and Wenham base their interpretation on the location of this clause in the sentence. They note that it could have been in one of three places:

1. Between "whoever" and "divorces."

2. Between "his wife" and "and marries another."

3. Between "marries another" and "commits adultery."

They state that if it were in the first position, it would make divorce mandatory in case of sexual immorality, but I agree with Luck that it is hard to see how this could be. The fact is that all that first position would do in Greek grammar would be to emphasize the exception clause. It would be like underlining the clause or placing it in italics.

(It would be possible to get the meaning Heth and Wenham suggest if, instead of moving the whole clause, one moves only the word *me* (not), but this is not what they said. They spoke of moving the "exception clause.")

They state that putting the exception clause at the third position would have made it mean what Erasmus said, that if the divorce is valid before God, then remarriage is permissible also. However, even after long consideration, it is impossible for me to see that the sentence would have any meaning at all if the exception clause came in that third position. It would be saying that the remarriage was done "because of adultery." But what could that possibly mean? Why would anyone marry another person because his first wife committed some sexual immorality? It makes no sense. I think Heth and Wenham were trying too hard to find support for their theory that even if divorce is sometimes permitted by God, remarriage never is.

Dr. Wilber T. Dayton, formerly a professor at Asbury Seminary, and later at Wesley Biblical Seminary, also disagrees with Heth and Wenham. On this point he writes:

Divorce and remarriage are a sequence taken together, because they naturally fit together. They cannot be separated in the parallel construction in this passage. If the principle is that the divorce and remarriage are adultery, as seems entirely clear, then the exception clause exempts both from the charge of adultery. That is, it would be wrong to infer from this verse that Jesus permitted a man to innocently divorce his wife, but that the adultery would be in the remarriage. Both elements of the parallelism must be treated the same. We are not told which is the greater sin—the divorce or the remarriage. That is not the present point. Both are sinful except where neither is sinful (Dayton, Caldwell, and Schultz 1984).

THE MEANING OF *PORNEIA*

The word *porneia* is here translated "adultery." There have been other suggestions: (1) Some have suggested it means only pre-marital sex with another person. (2) Some have suggested it refers only to incest. But there is no support for either of these, though the word could include those ideas. It does not normally refer to such ideas, but rather to extra-marital sex, and is probably as broad in meaning as "sexual immorality." It could include adultery, homosexuality, incest, prostitution, or sexual perversions, as can be seen by its uses in the Septuagint (Greek version of the Old Testament).

The point of insisting that *porneia* has some narrow meaning such as "incest" or "premarital infidelity" is that such a meaning would make the statement of Jesus apply, not to divorce after marriage, but to the breaking of an engagement. But if that were true, Jesus missed the point of the question, or he would not have called attention to Deuteronomy 24. Since he did do this, it is evident that he was not considering the breaking off of an engagement, but rather of the ending of a consummated marriage in divorce. The Pharisees were asking about the legitimate grounds for divorce.

They spent their time quibbling about the meaning of that which made divorce possible. But this is not the point of emphasis in what Jesus said. Jesus put the emphasis back where it belonged all along—on the permanence of marriage. He showed what was truly important. Instead of discussing the grounds on which a man could legitimately divorce his wife, as they were doing, Jesus insisted on returning to the creation plan of God to make marriage a life-long commitment. Divorce was permitted by Moses only to prevent hardhearted men from driving their wives away with no means of resisting and no way of continuing to support themselves.

9

REMARRIAGE IN
THE GOSPELS

Heth and Wenham take the position that marriage following divorce is always adulterous, no matter what the grounds for the divorce. So they insist that even though divorce is possible under certain circumstances, it is never right for the divorced person to marry another. They support this by three lines of reasoning.

a. Argument from Greek grammar. Their reasoning here is not easy to follow. It is built on the concept mentioned above that the position of the exception clause affects its meaning. They insist that the position of the clause in the sentence makes any remarriage absolutely forbidden no matter what the cause of the divorce.

But I agree with others that this reasoning makes no sense, and that the clause is in the only natural position in the sentence. None of their attempts to illustrate their grammatical analysis help, since they are not truly parallel to this sentence. The fact is that this is the only sentence of its kind in the New Testament. There is nothing to which it can be compared.

b. The argument of eternal oneness. The concept here is that the oneness of the married persons is of a spiritual or metaphysical nature and is eternal. This oneness, some have insisted, can never be broken, and this means that any other marriage would be adultery, even if the first spouse had died. Here Heth and Wenham are following Isaacson.

However, this seems to be reading more into the biblical expression than is implied. Surely such an interpretation is not explicit anywhere in the Bible. Further, "one flesh" is not the same as "one spirit." And since Jesus said there will be no marriage in heaven, this unity cannot be eternal, but only for this life. It is a way of expressing the proper intention of God for the couple to remain one for life. It is a symbol of the couple's commitment to live and work together as one. It is this intention, rather than any kind of metaphysical oneness. Just as two horses become one team, so the two persons become one couple. But in the case of the marriage, the persons enter into this oneness by a choice and a voluntary commitment.

THE PURPOSE OF JESUS

Luck is illuminating on this aspect. In his study of this passage, he analyzes the two major theories about the purpose of the Pharisees and suggests a third, which seems good to me. Briefly, he points out first the problems with the common statement that the Pharisees were trying to get Jesus to side with either Hillel or Shammai, two groups of Pharisees. But trapping Jesus would do the Pharisees no good, since some Pharisees would agree and some would disagree. A second suggestion is that the trap was to get Jesus involved in the Herod versus John the Baptist affair. Yet this would not help them get Jesus out of the way and might hurt the Pharisees more than Jesus.

Luck suggests that what they were really trying to do was to get Jesus to deny the law of Moses, thus turning the people against him. And since Jesus had already stated antipathy to divorce (Luke 16:18), they thought they could get him to say something they could use against him. As Luck shows by his analysis of the conversation, this supposition of their purpose makes good sense out of the description given by Matthew.

Jesus avoided the trap and supported the law, but at the same time he emphasized the error of divorce. He strongly stated that marriage was intended by God to be for all of life and that divorce is a failure to make it work.

When Jesus said that the divorce law was given because of the hardness of hearts, he was not saying that God changed his mind and approved divorce. He was saying rather that if a man was hard hearted enough to want to get rid of his wife, God protected the rights of the wife by the law given in Deuteronomy 24:1-4.

For that is exactly what the law does—it protects the rights of the wife. It does not in any way alter God's original intent for marriage to be for life.

The law of Moses was saying to the husband who wanted to divorce his wife that he had better think carefully about what he was considering. If he did divorce her, he would have to give some consideration to her needs and not just send her away as would an Egyptian. He would have to do it legally and would have to prove in court that there was some sufficient reason. Then he would have to give her a properly drawn up certificate of divorce so that she would be free to remarry or otherwise take care of herself. All this was necessary, as Jesus pointed out, because of the hardness of the human heart, since men did not naturally do what was right for the wife.

So we see that Jesus avoided any appearance of voiding or altering the law of Moses. Yet at the same time he upheld the permanence of marriage and stressed that it is not God's will for marriage to end in divorce. He gave the Pharisees no handle by which to hurt his ministry, though he showed them their error.

The problem of remarriage is not solved by any explicit statement in the New Testament. Mark and Luke indicate Jesus gave mission for divorce in the case of adultery, but they do not mention remarriage. So they give no guidance on this. Matthew gives us the further implication that Jesus, in such a case, permitted divorce. It would seem logical that, if the divorce is truly valid in the sight of God, then God would also sanction remarriage, if prayerfully planned. If this is true, then any remarriage should be considered on the same basis of commitment to the will of God which should characterize a first marriage.

Remarriage should be entered into only with fear and trembling and much prayer. One should use all the insights gained through the first marriage and divorce in making any plans for or against remarriage.

There is no specific statement in the New Testament that remarriage is permissible in any and all cases. But the strong emphasis on God's plan for marriage to be for life is a warning against a casual view of divorce and remarriage.

ANOTHER SUGGESTED SOLUTION

It has been suggested by some persons that there are two Hebrew and Greek words with different meanings. These persons state that one of the words (Greek *apoluo*) means to "send away without divorce" and that the other (Greek *apostasion*) means "divorce." Although several writers mention the theory, the only discussion I have found like this is by the Rev. Walter Callison (*Your Church*, Evanston, Illinois: Your Church Publications, May/June, 1986). He states that the Pharisees and lawyers who came to Jesus asked if it was right to send a wife away without divorce, but that Jesus insisted that one must actually divorce her instead.

It is true that there are the two words in Greek, but one is a verb *(apoluein)* and the other a noun *(apostasion)*. The Greek verb *apostasiazo*, which could presumably mean "to divorce," is never used in the New Testament nor in the Septuagint of the Old Testament. So the situation we have is that the Bible uses *apoluein* to mean "to divorce" and *apostosaion* to mean "a divorce certificate." The most common phrase is *biblion apostasion*, which means a "certificate of divorce." *Apostasion* is not, and cannot be, used by itself to mean "to divorce" someone. The noun is used only three times in the New Testament (Matt. 5:31; 19:7; Mark 10:4).

In Matthew 5:31, the full phrase "bill of divorcement" is not used, but it clearly refers to the official certificate, as it does in the other places and in the Septuagint. The *Greek Grammar of the New Testament* documents the word in classical Greek as meaning the certificate of divorce. The same lexicon states that *apoluein* means "to divorce" a wife or husband (Chicago: University of Chicago Press, 1961).

Since the Greek *luo* means "to loose or destroy," it is easy to see how *apoluo* could come to mean "to divorce, to break or destroy the contract of marriage." The natural way to say "send away" would be *exapostello* or *ekballo* or *aphieme*. Moulton and Milligan (J. H. Moulton and G. Milligan. *The Vocabularly of the Greek New Testament*. Grand Rapids: Eerdmans, 1930) state that the most common use of *apoluein* is "to divorce a wife or husband." When a Jewish man divorced (Hebrew *shalach*, Greek *apoluo*) his wife he had to give her a certificate of divorce (Hebrew *sepher kerithuth*, Greek *biblion apostasia*). This is exactly what is stated in Malachi 2:16; Mark 10:4; Matthew 5:31; and Deuteronomy 24. Both words are used in the same clause.

Also in Matthew 1:19, Joseph, being a just *(dikaios)* man, decided to *apolusai* Mary. Following to Callison's theory would mean Joseph wanted to "send her away" instead of divorcing her!

The proof of our interpretation is in the conversation as recorded in Matthew, who has the fullest account of it. If we assume that *apolusai* means "to send away without divorce," I find it hard to understand what Jesus said in Matthew 19:8. After they said, "Why then did Moses command to give a bill of divorce and send her away?" Jesus said to them, "Moses, for the hardness of your hearts, permitted you to send away (apolusai) your wives. From the beginning it was not so." In that case, Jesus agreed that Moses permitted them to send away their wives without divorce. That would contradict Deuteronomy 24.

The fact is clear, then, that Jesus supported the Old Testament law that if a man was determined to divorce his wife, he had to give her written proof of the divorce. This was for the protection of the wife.

And it is just as clear that neither the Old Testament nor Jesus was in favor of divorce. The Bible never commands divorce and never says that God was pleased with divorce. God wills for marriage to be for all of life. But God tolerates divorce in this sinful world. At the same time, God insists that if one divorces, he or she must show proper concern for the one being divorced.

When the Pharisees sought to show that Jesus was opposed to the Old Testament law, he did not simply answer with a yes or no. He pointed out that the will of God was to be sought in the very beginning of the Old Testament. He took them back to the story of creation itself and showed that God's plan has always been for lifelong marriage — not for divorce.

10

THE TEACHING OF PAUL

Paul nowhere discusses divorce. Two passages (Rom. 7:1-3 and 1 Cor. 7) have been used in modern discussions, but in neither of them does Paul discuss divorce in general or give the proper grounds for divorce. He puts the emphasis just where Jesus had put it—on the life-long permanence of marriage.

Romans 7:1-3

Note how Paul uses the permanence of marriage until death to illustrate the fact that sin has power over a person until that person dies:

Do you not know, brothers—for I am speaking to men who know the law—that the law has authority over a man only as long as he lives? For example, by law a married woman is bound to her husband as long as he is alive, but if her husband dies, she is released from the law of marriage. So then, if she marries another man while her husband is still alive, she is called an adulteress. But if her husband dies, she is released from that law and is not an adulteress, even though she marries another man.

Death dissolves the marriage. It is possible to conclude from this passage that only death can dissolve a marriage. But it is never proper to isolate one passage from all the rest of the Bible. As we have seen, Jesus and the Old Testament showed that divorce can dissolve a marriage for sufficient reason. So we see that Paul here is simply using the permanence of marriage to illustrate the way in which sin can control a person as long as he or she is under its power and authority. One can die to sin in Christ and be free from sin's power.

Paul here is discussing only the way in which death ends a marriage, and says nothing about divorce. He is using marriage only as an illustration, and divorce has nothing to do with the point he is making. So it is a complete mistake for some to use this passage, which is really an analogy, to support a theory that a marriage can never be dissolved except by death.

1 Corinthians 7

Before considering the details of the relevant parts of 1 Corinthians 7, we need to note that there is a major problem in this chapter—we do not know for sure what Paul is talking about in some passages. We simply do not know much about the situation in Corinth or the exact questions with which Paul was dealing. For that reason, scholars have written extensively on their various theories about this chapter. Who were the men who "had" virgins? Why was there a problem with their marriage? What was the "impending distress?"

In this chapter Paul writes in response to certain questions which were sent to him in a letter we do not have. So we do not know exactly how the questions about marriage were worded. This makes for certain difficulty in understanding what Paul means. So we should be cautious in our exposition. But if we are careful, we can come to an exposition which will disagree neither with what Paul teaches elsewhere nor with the rest of the Bible.

In the first six chapters, Paul wrote about some of the problems in the church at Corinth. He had been pastor in that pagan city and knew from the correspondence some of the problems which had developed after he left. Now in chapter 7 he begins to deal with some of the specific questions which they had sent to him. The first question was about marriage. Paul led up to this question by a discussion of sexual immorality in 6:12-20. Then he writes: Now for the matters you wrote about: It is good for a man not to marry. But since there is so much immorality, each man should have his own wife, and each woman her own husband" (7:1-3).

"It is good for a man not to touch a woman." That is the way the King James Version puts it. But this expression is a euphemism for sexual relations, as the footnote in the NIV says and as most commentators agree. Paul does not say that it is better not to marry, but that it is good and honorable. It would be a mistake to say that Paul was opposed to marriage, as is clear from the fact that in Ephesians 5:25-33 he uses marriage to illustrate the relationship between Christ and the church. This shows the exalted view which Paul held of marriage.

This second part of the first verse has occasioned more than its share of discussion. One thing is clear. Paul was not saying that it is more spiritual to be single than to be married. In the first place, that would contradict the whole teaching of the Bible about sex and marriage. Second, in verses 3-5 of this same chapter, Paul insists that sexual relations in marriage should not be neglected. Finally, some scholars have suggested that Paul was here quoting his questioners in Corinth in order to introduce the discussion. (See the discussion of this verse by A. D. Verhey in *International Standard Bible Encyclopedia*, edited by Geoffrey W. Bromiley, Grand Rapids: Eerdmans, 1979, 1:978.) The reason for this statement was that there were some in the church at Corinth who denied any future resurrection. Probably they believed as did some in Philippi that our spiritual resurrection in Christ is all the resurrection there is. So we are already like the angels and should not marry.

Paul agrees with them that it might be good not to marry, but for an entirely different reason—"because of the impending distress" (1 Cor. 7:26. *Amplified Bible*. Grand Rapids: Zondervan, 1958). We do not know what kind of distress Paul means, but it was no mystery to the Corinthians.

It seems that some of the Corinthians must have misunderstood the teaching of Paul about sexual relations and thought he meant that all sex is wrong. In view of the pagan atmosphere in which they lived, this is not surprising. They had trouble distinguishing between legitimate sexual relations and illegitimate. In their pagan state, there had been no real difference. So when they had been told that extramarital sex was wrong, many of them concluded that there was something wrong and unchristian about sex, and so they ought to be celibate.

Verse 2 uses an unusual plural in the Greek: "because of the immoralities." This was not a misleading way of saying what was going on in such a pagan place as Corinth, and it would be fitting in America today. Paul recognizes the fact that living in the midst of such immorality makes for multiple temptations. Extramarital relationships were an accepted part of men's lives, and going to a religious prostitute was considered a proper part of pagan worship. Marriage was primarily for the sake of having legitimate children.

Faithfulness in the man was not expected. So Paul points out the simple fact that for each to have his or her own wife or husband can be an advantage to purity, as well as a witness to a pagan world. The Christians in Corinth needed to understand that marriage is not wrong. What happens when people are told that having sexual relations is sinful and that no one ought to get married is that a person may refrain from sex in marriage and then go to prostitutes. A psychologist can explain why this happens. Judging from what Paul had written in 6:12-20, that is what some had already done in Corinth. Paul had to set them straight.

Paul made it clear that there is no excellence in married celibacy. Celibacy is honorable, but so is marriage. And there must be no polygamy. God planned for one husband and one wife.

1 Corinthians 7:4-9

In verses 4-6 Paul explains that sexual relations in marriage are good and natural and do not frustrate the spiritual development of the persons.

In verse 7 Paul makes a statement which has often been misunderstood. "I wish that all men were as I am. But each man has his own gift from God: one has this gift, another has that." It is clear that Paul was unmarried at this time, though we do not know whether he was ever married or not. He was either a widower, as some believe, or had never been married. He knows the advantages of this unmarried state for himself in his work and could wish that all were single also. But he recognizes that all are not alike. Jesus had said that celibacy is not for everyone but is only for those to whom God gave that gift (Matt. 19:11-12). Paul is expressing the same thought in different words in verse 7, and he continues this thought in the next two verses. If one has the gift of single living, and if that is the best way for that person to serve God, then it is good not to be married. But if not, then that person should not think he or she is doing any wrong to be married.

In this connection, it is wise to remind ourselves that Paul is not discussing marriage in general in this chapter. He is discussing marriage in a particular situation. He is discussing it with people who had pagan ideas of sex and marriage which needed correction. And he is discussing it in answer to a specific set of questions which had been raised by the church in Corinth. So we should be careful about any general application of his words.

1 Corinthians 7:10-16

In this passage, Paul is addressing the serious problems encountered by a Christian whose husband or wife is still a pagan. No doubt there were many such couples in the churches of cities like Corinth. Probably some thought such Christians ought to leave their pagan companions because of the difficulties in living in such a pagan environment. Paul says that it is better for them not to leave, but rather they should stay with the partner. He suggests that the example of the Christian might even bring the pagan partner to salvation. In such a case, the pagan would be "sanctified" by the Christian partner's influence, and the children, too, can be saved through Christian influence and teaching.

We do not so commonly have the same situation in this country today, but we have many marriages in which one is saved and the other is not. Paul says this is not reason enough for divorce, so long as the unsaved partner is willing to stay. If the unsaved person is not willing to stay in the marriage, then Paul says this does not bring guilt to the saved partner.

In thinking of applying these words to any modern situation, we must remind ourselves that Paul was dealing with an uncommon problem. Except for converted Jews, all of the Christians in the church at Corinth were newly converted from various pagan, idol-worshiping religions. When only one marriage partner was converted, there was a serious problem which could lead one or both of them to consider divorce. This is what led to the writing of chapter seven of Paul's letter.

This situation is far different from that of mixed marriages where one is a Christian and the other is not. A Christian ought to be careful to stay out of such a situation. A sinner can be converted, and a Christian can go back into sin, thus leading to a problem. But even then, it is not just what the Corinthian Christians were facing. So Paul was dealing with a special and difficult circumstance.

Paul says that in such a situation the Christian should not divorce the pagan (vs. 10, 12-13). It is better to stay together with the pagan and trust that the partner may be converted. Paul gives three reasons for this: (1) The unbeliever is sanctified through the partner (v. 14). (2) God has called us to live in peace (v. 15). (3) You may save your partner (v. 16).

This first reason raises problems. How can it be said that a person is "sanctified" by the Christian marriage partner? He explains his reason for this statement by saying that "otherwise your children would be unclean, but as it is, they are holy." We can understand this if we note that Paul, with his rabbinic training, is using two words (unclean and holy) in their Old Testament ceremonial sense. A person or thing which is unclean is not fit to be presented to God for his use. The person or thing has first to be cleansed of the uncleanness. Uncleanness had to do especially with anything associated with idol worship, which is worship of anything other than God. This cleansing from pagan uncleanness is what Paul means here by "sanctified." If the Christian leaves the pagan with the children, they will grow up pagan, with little chance of ever being saved. Further, the Christian will then lose all chance of helping convert the other.

The second reason Paul gives is easy to understand. He says that we are called to live in peace with others, rather than unnecessarily upsetting relationships. So the Christian ought to seek to make the non-Christian partner happy and to influence the other for good. It is only in this way that the Christian can hope to bring the other person to Christ, which ought to be the goal.

Now it is in connection with the salvation of the marriage partner that verse 11 can be understood. He has remarked that the Christian wife should not leave her husband. "But if she does, she must remain unmarried or else be reconciled to her husband. And a husband must not divorce his wife." This has sometimes been used to reject all remarriage for Christians. But Paul's point seems to be that remarriage would mean the end of the Christian's hope of reconciliation to the former partner by that partner's conversion. This conversion of the other, and consequent reconciliation, is the goal for which one should strive. Marriage to another would make it impossible.

Some have suggested that we should make a distinction between the two words Paul and Jesus used for "divorce." The idea is that one of them means actual legal divorce, and the other means merely separation. It is true that there are few if any true synonyms in any language, since there are always certain differences in connotation, if not denotation. But it seems clear that they are used synonymously. Both *chorizo* and *apolyo* are used in such a way that they can hardly mean less than divorce. In this we see the agreement of the lexicons and most commentators.

1 Corinthians 7:17-25

"Nevertheless, each one should retain the place in life that the Lord assigned to him and to which God has called him. This is the rule I lay down in all the churches" (v. 17). Paul gives now the general rule, of which he has just given a specific application, followed by more applications. The person's station in life does not need to be changed when one is saved, unless there is something inherently sinful in what is being done. If a person is circumcised or uncircumcised, slave or free, when converted, those circumstances do not interfere with pleasing God as a Christian. So one need not seek to change it. The Corinthians had thoroughly misunderstood the Christian attitude toward marriage; they felt that it was sinful for a Christian to be married to a non-Christian and that perhaps it was better for a Christian not to be married at all. This is what Paul had to clear up.

1 Corinthians 7:39

Death dissolves the marriage. The same point is made here as in Romans 7. But here Paul is discussing marriage itself, and not simply using marriage to illustrate a point. However, he goes on here to point out that the living spouse is free to remarry after the death of the other. This latter point demolishes the concept that remarriage is never valid or right.

SUMMARY OF PAUL'S TEACHING

So Paul is stressing the permanence of marriage as the basic Christian principle. Yet at the same time he is recognizing the problems which can exist in this kind of world. Dobson summarizes the teaching of Paul in this passage in four principles (1986, 82):

1. He advocates permanence in the marriage relationship (7:39-40).

2. He advocates the reconciliation of divorced and separated parties (7:10-11).

3. He permits divorce on the grounds of religious differences (7:15).

4. He permits remarriage after a legitimate divorce (7:28).

11

DIVORCE AND REMARRIAGE IN HISTORY

In the study of any teaching of the Bible, it is helpful to know how the church has interpreted that doctrine through the last two thousand years. We must not slavishly adopt what was taught in any particular period of history or by any particular person. But we can always learn something of the present concepts by learning how they came to be. If we come to understand what others have believed, and when and why those beliefs have been adopted and later changed, we can know better how to evaluate our own ideas.

THE INTERPRETATION OF ERASMUS

Since Heth and Wenham give considerable attention to what they call the "Erasmian theory" or interpretation of divorce and remarriage, we need to be clear as to their meaning. The primary thrust of the book by these two authors is that the Christian church has been led astray by the exegesis of Erasmus and must return to the pre-Reformation concept that divorce means separation only and that remarriage is never acceptable to God.

To say this may be putting too much responsibility on Erasmus. They did not necessarily copy Erasmus, who was an older contemporary of Luther, but they came to the same conclusions he did and for some of the same reasons. Luther and Calvin rejected the Roman Catholic teachings because they determined they were unscriptural.

We need to examine the situation in the sixteenth century. Heth and Wenham emphasize the fact that the Roman Catholic church was teaching that divorce was wrong and that remarriage was never proper if the first marriage partner was still living. That is true, but that is not the real problem.

By the beginning of the fifteenth century the church was teaching the unbiblical concept that celibacy is better and more spiritual than marriage. This rests partly on the pagan Greek assumption that sin has its seat and source in the body and that only the soul can be holy. Therefore, the physical pleasure of the body in marriage was considered to be less spiritual, an evil to be tolerated in laymen but not in the clergy. Therefore, clergy were not to be married. (This was true in the Roman Catholic church, but the Eastern Orthodox Church had from the beginning allowed their clergy to be married.)

It is clear that the Bible does not teach this, either in the Old Testament or in the New; God commanded human beings in the beginning to be fruitful and multiply. Marriage should be "honored by all" (Heb. 13:4). In 1 Timothy 4:3, one of the doctrines of devils is to "forbid people to marry." Further, both in the Old and New Testaments, marriage is made the symbol of the relation between God and his people. So the Church, like Israel before, is called the bride of Christ.

THE EARLY CHURCH

It is amazing how quickly this heretical prejudice against marriage came into the church. Many of the early church fathers (Ignatius, Justin Martyr, Tatian, Origen and Tertullian) felt that marriage was not as good and holy as celibacy. Each of them, to a greater or less degree, felt that celibacy was a better and higher state than marriage. Jerome was fanatical in his denunciation of marriage, and Augustine was very much a part of his age in this respect. It is not surprising that Heth and Wenham could quote most of these men as opposing remarriage. They had a low view of marriage in the first place! So they opposed any second marriage.

At the same time, some of these men, such as Origen and Tertullian, for example, did permit divorce and remarriage in certain cases. Their prohibition was not absolute.

Further, it is not easy to know exactly what these early writers really believed, as they did not write systematic treatises but dealt with specific problems as they arose. Justin Martyr, for instance, condemned remarriage in certain passages but did not in certain other passages. (For further study, see Luck 1987, 2:55-270.)

Augustine taught in more than one place that neither of the persons after divorce could contract a new marriage. However, in his "Retractions" he expresses doubt on this subject. It must be recognized that one of his reasons for denouncing remarriage was that he was concerned about the welfare of divorced women.

Rare as it may be, some workers in the church may have work to do which can be better done by a single person than by a married couple. So there are times when marriage is not expedient for a particular person. Jesus pointed out to his disciples that some "have renounced marriage because of the kingdom of heaven" (Matt. 19:12). One wonders, for instance, if Paul would have been quite as free to do his traveling ministry if he had been married. Yet he declared that he had as much right as Peter and others to have a wife, but he refrained for the sake of his work in the churches (1 Cor. 9:5).

THE ROMAN CATHOLIC TEACHING

In spite of the later doubts of Augustine,

the Roman Catholic church developed a theology which excluded divorce. This was strengthened by the theology of sacraments as ceremonies which truly bestow grace upon the participants. When marriage was declared to be a sacrament, which conferred divine grace on the two persons, then divorce was made impossible.

But this left some people in intolerable situations, and so over the years the church developed a list of sixteen causes for nullification of marriage. If a person wanted out of a marriage, the only way was to show to the satisfaction of the church that one of the causes applied. Most of these were impediments to a valid marriage so that the church could rule that the marriage had not been valid in the first place. It seems clear that these causes for annulment of marriage are merely a substitute for divorce, which had been ruled out when marriage was declared to be a sacrament. Besides these causes for annulment, there were a list of causes for separation without divorce.

THE REFORMERS

It was this method of annulment of marriages, with its resultant abuses, which led to the revolt of the reformers against the Roman Catholic view of marriage and divorce. If a marriage had fallen apart to such an extent that the partners wanted out of it, the only way, since a divorce could not be sanctioned by the church, was to get an annulment.

Thus, they had to show that one of the sixteen "impediments" applied, showing that they could not have been properly married in the first place. If they succeeded in this, then the marriage was annulled and the church announced that the marriage had never taken place.

It is not difficult to see how this could lead to multiple abuses, with couples searching for some way to apply one of the "impediments" to their marriage. It was the rich and famous who were most often able to succeed in getting an annulment. This whole system seemed false and wrong to persons such as Luther and Calvin, and they rebelled against it. They felt that it was more honest and more scriptural to admit the reality of divorce under some scriptural conditions than to make such a long and unscriptural list of reasons for annulment, which could be applied no matter how long the couple had been married. It is better to admit what the Bible says, that a marriage can be broken by adultery after it is properly performed. This the reformers declared.

Calvin points out the falsehood of calling marriage a sacrament and then refusing to let the clergy participate in it. He was attempting to show that the Roman Catholic concept was not according to Scripture. Actually, Calvin showed that the whole concept was based on their low view of marriage.

THE MODERN CHURCH

Since the Reformation, the church has continued to stress the will of God for marriage to be permanent, as the Bible says. Yet there have been adaptations to the breakdown of marriages which have led to the permission for divorce in too many cases. This tendency has gotten out of hand in the last half-century. Even in the evangelical and fundamentalist churches, divorce and remarriage have come to be tolerated, if not accepted as normal.

What this means is that it is time for a revival of marriage as a lifetime commitment. It is time for the church to seek ways to help Christians build stronger marriages. The biblical teaching is clear and is a mandate to the church.

12

DIVORCED AND
REMARRIED PASTORS

In considering the teaching of Paul on divorce and remarriage, we find that he wrote some special directions to pastors. If we are to know all the Bible teaches on this subject, it is necessary to look at some of these carefully.

We understand that every pastor is first of all a human being. He or she is chosen to do a special work in the church, but has the same needs and problems others face. The pastor can get discouraged as others do, and faces temptations as much as any Christian does. And the pastor can have problems in marriage, and may even be divorced. In this latter case, the congregation needs to understand the teaching of the Bible on the divorce of a pastor, so as to help both the pastor and the congregation. For that reason we will consider here the passages which are directed to the pastor and his marriage.

In several passages, Paul lists some of the

requirements for a pastor. One of those requirements is that he should be "the husband of one wife" (1 Tim. 3:2; Titus 1:6). It can be seen that this applies both to deacons in general and to pastors. No one should be too dogmatic about these passages, since there is so much disagreement among scholars as to their exact meaning.

The statement "husband of one wife" does rule out polygamy or having more than one wife at a time. But there was little or no polygamy in Greece at the time of Paul, so why should this be the main thrust of Paul's statement?

On the other hand, it might be intended to rule out remarriage after divorce for pastors and deacons. Some of the early church fathers believed this, but others disagreed. Probably most of them opposed remarriage—not primarily on account of this passage, but because they had adopted a philosophy which thought of celibacy as more spiritual than marriage. So they felt it would be better not to be married even once. However, this attitude is not supported in either Old or New Testament.

It has been suggested that this statement may rule out the unmarried pastor, as though it said "at least one wife." But the Greek sentence would not naturally have this meaning.

If these suggestions are not to be thought of as the true meaning of Paul's admonition, then it would be helpful to look more closely at the passage. It is then seen that the passage could be translated "a one-woman man." The Greek expression is arranged so that it puts emphasis on the "one." Thus, this would mean "not a womanizer." It would agree with 2 Peter 2:14: not having "eyes full of adultery." The pastor must act circumspectly toward women, just as every Christian should. But the pastor has more responsibility to live to the very highest standard because of his public position as an overseer. He should be an example of the finest Christian character, if he is to lead others.

John Wesley, in his first annual conference for his assistants, gave twelve rules for them to follow. The first was: "Be diligent." The second was: "Be serious. Let your motto be, 'holiness unto the Lord.'"

Then the third: "Touch no woman. Be as loving as you will but hold your hands off of them. Custom is nothing to us." (Quoted in Albert C. Outler, *John Wesley*. New York: Oxford University Press, 1964, p. 145.)

Many will consider this to be extreme, and it may be. But there are two considerations we should think about. The first is that John Wesley found too many of his young ministers falling into sexual sins and dropping out of the work. So he had to warn the others. The second reason is that what is considered by one to be an innocent touch may be taken as not so innocent by another. One cannot be too careful at this point. It is wiser to seem to be a little distant with women than to be too free with them.

A further reason for this kind of care is the advice Paul gave to Timothy in 1 Timothy 5:1-2: "Do not rebuke an older man harshly, but exhort him as if he were your father. Treat younger men as brothers, older women as mothers, and younger women as sisters, with absolute purity."

This is advice which every pastor ought to take seriously from the time he first begins his work. All of the advice is good, and the way we are to treat women is a means to prevent much of the trouble pastors have.

SOME PERSONAL OBSERVATIONS

a. In my half-century in the ministry I have seen too many pastors fall. Some have been divorced to marry another. Some have committed adultery. Almost all of them have blamed their wives for their own divorce or adultery. "My wife was unloving." "My wife just did not want to be a preacher's wife." These statements I have heard over and over. I do not think I have ever heard a pastor, caught in adultery, say he was to blame.

b. Adultery can be forgiven but only after sincere repentance and an attempt to mend all hurts and make any restitution possible.

c. If a divorced person marries soon after the divorce, it looks as though the divorce was for the purpose of marrying another.

d. A pastor is to live blameless in the community. What may be accepted in the community in a lay person or another professional may not be accepted in a pastor.

e. Divorce is always a sign of failure, since God's plan is for no divorce. A pastor who divorces will have to live with that failure. He or she will be forever handicapped in dealing with marital troubles in others.

f. Even if divorced pastors feel they have the "right" to go on pastoring the church, they should consider their responsibility to the church and may come to a different conclusion. As Paul pointed out, some things may be permitted which are not expedient or beneficial (1 Cor. 10:23). "Nobody should seek his own good, but the good of others" (v. 24).

HELMUT THIELECKE

On the matter of divorced and remarried pastors, one of the best discussions I have read is by the German theologian/pastor Helmut Thielecke in a brief section at the end of a chapter on divorce and remarriage. Thielecke argues that even if the pastor is totally innocent so far as the cause of the divorce is concerned, he is less able to serve others as pastor.

To hear the words ". . . till death us do part" spoken as a vow by one who himself could not or did not satisfy that obligation can provoke offense and seriously increase the already threatening danger that the church's blessing will be misunderstood as a mere conventional ceremony. If, however, the pastor has been guilty of a breakdown in his marriage that is discernible and reprehensible to men, then . . . the respect of the church for the institution of marriage demands that it no longer permit him to exercise his office in its name. . . .

But even in the case where from the legal point of view the minister is the "innocent" party in the divorce . . . he is in a position where the facts as they are now known to the public . . . are at the mercy of whatever interpretation the public may put upon them . . . he has no possibility of . . . preventing them from casting doubt upon the credibility of his office and his message. . . .

Therefore in every case—including cases where the minister is declared "innocent" in civil law—it is obvious that the minister must give up his office and should be urged to do so. If, for whatever reasons, this conclusion is not drawn, then at least a transfer is unavoidable. (*Theological Ethics*, translated by John W. Doberstein. Grand Rapids: William B. Eerdmans Publishing Co., 1964. 3:176-177.)

Dr. Thielecke means that in some cases the pastor might be able to serve a different church where his past might not hinder him, though he seems to say this rather reluctantly. He does conclude by saying that the church should not hinder such a pastor from serving in some other form of ministry.

HELPING THE TROUBLED PASTOR

When a pastor is having marriage problems or getting a divorce, his congregation needs to pray earnestly for their pastor. They need to do whatever they can to encourage both pastor and spouse. They must not hastily take sides, or try to solve the pastor's problem. But they can seek to be supportive, and give time for matters to be worked out. Some things need to be left to the pastor and the ministers of the area to solve.

The church at large must continue to search for ways to help pastors in their marriages, and to minister to those whose marriages fail. The failure may or may not be the fault of the pastor, but he or she needs healing. And so does the congregation. It should not be left to the congregation alone to decide what to do with a pastor who has gone through a divorce. This places a burden on them which they are not trained or prepared to handle.

The ministers of the area need to think through the problem, and pray for grace and guidance from God in handling each situation. Each problem is different, and no blanket rule is adequate. The desire should be to bring healing to all persons concerned. But real healing cannot come unless we follow biblical principles. It is not enough to say that we must forgive. Easy forgiveness, with no godly sorrow, is simply condoning, and is not helpful to any of the persons involved. Yet to seek to do more than this is to lay ourselves and others open to real pain. This painful course is the only way out.

13

GENERAL CONCLUSIONS

1. It is God's will for one man to marry one woman for life.

2. Divorce is never a part of God's ideal plan, and it never has been.

3. Divorce is sometimes "permitted" by God because of human failure to attain the ideal. But it never is according to God's plan.

4. Jesus "permits divorce" when adultery has already disrupted the marriage.

5. Though adultery legally is the act itself, the New Testament is not concerned with legal legislation, but rather with basic principles of ethics. It is more concerned with the intention of the heart than with overt actions.

6. Adultery does not make divorce imperative, only permissible. Even sin against a marriage can be forgiven. Adultery does not make a Christian marriage impossible after it is repented of and discontinued.

7. When a marriage union is not viable, God permits the dissolution of that marriage.

When a married person has sexual relations with someone other than the marriage partner, he or she has been untrue to his or her marriage partner and marriage vows. That sin dissolves the union, and the innocent partner is free to divorce the unfaithful spouse and remarry.

"When a person becomes so untrue to his companion and false to his marriage vow as to have sexual relations with another person, God allows such an unchaste sin, and such a sin only, to dissolve the union. In token of that link being broken, the innocent party may divorce the guilty and enter into another marriage."

8. If marriage is truly ended by divorce, and this divorce is valid before God, then one has freedom to remarry. Such remarriage should be careful and prayerful, not casual. Augustine, and some earlier fathers, denied the validity of remarriage, but this is because he was influenced against marriage by Greek philosophy that the body is sinful. Hodge (*Systematic Theology*, 3:396-7) argues that if death ends a marriage and permits remarriage, then desertion does the same, as it too is final separation. But he insists rightly that incompatibility of temperament does not.

H. Orton Wiley (*Christian Theology*, 3:19-85) quotes Hodge at length on this subject and closely follows his reasoning with approval.

9. A divorced person may be a Christian (1 Cor. 6:9-11). God can save people who di-

vorced for reasons other than adultery and married again while in sin and ignorance of the Bible teaching.

10. There were in the Corinthian church men who had more than one woman to whom they had been married; and they were not told to separate from the last wife and go back to the first wife in order to be saved.

11. Divorce is always in some sense a failure, always to be deplored and to be avoided if at all possible.

12. Some marriages end in failure because they should never have been made. Even if the problem is insoluble, the Christian involved must seek self-understanding, repentance, and guidance for the future.

13. Divorce leaves life-long scars, no matter what the circumstances.

14. When a divorced person wishes to remarry, some questions need to be asked:

    a. How long ago was the divorce?
    b. Is there no hope of reconciliation?
    c. What children are involved?
    d. In what way can God best be glorified in the future?
    e. How can the persons best win the confidence of others?
    f. What persons are involved, and what is their attitude?
    g. Has there been repentance for shortcomings and failure?

15. The major question to be answered is: "Can this couple build a Christian marriage together?" (This is the same question which

must be answered for any couple in their first marriage!)

16. Divorce, even in the best of circumstances, disqualifies one for some accomplishments that might otherwise have been made. Like suicide, divorce makes some things impossible. He or she can never reach the places of usefulness that might have been attained otherwise.

BIBLIOGRAPHY ON DIVORCE AND REMARRIAGE

Allmen, Jean Jacques, *Pauline Teaching on Marriage.* London: Faith Press, 1963.

Boutrager, G. Edwin, *Divorce and the Faithful Church.* Scottsdale, Pa: Herald Press, 1978. (Introduction by David Augsburger.)

Bromiley, Geoffrey W. *God and Marriage.* Grand Rapids: Eerdmans, 1980.

Crook, Roger H. *Bible Teachings on Marriage.* Nashville: Sunday School Board of Southern Baptist Convention. 1971.

Davies, W. W. "Divorce in the Old Testament," *International Standard Bible Encyclopedia.* 1939.

Dayton, Wilber T. Wayne E. Caldwell, and Carl Schultz. *Marriage—The Biblical Perspective.* Marion, Ind.: Wesley Press, 1984.

Dobson, Edward. "What the Bible Really Says about Marriage," *Divorce and Remarriage.* N. J.: Fleming H. Revell Co., 1986.

Duty, Guy. *Divorce and Remarriage.* Minneapolis: Bethany Fellowship, 1967.

Efird, James M. *Marriage and Divorce, What the Bible Says.* Nashville: Abingdon, 1985.

Ellison, Stanley E. *Divorce and Remarriage in the Church.* Grand Rapids: Zondervan Publishing House, 1977.

England, Harold Ray. Divorce and Remarriage in 1 Corinthians 7:10-16." Dissertation. Louisville, KY: Southern Baptist Seminary, 1982.

Epp, Theodore H. *God Speaks on Divorce.* Lincoln, Neb.: Back to the Bible Publisher, 1954.

Herron, Robert W., Jr. "Mark's Jesus on Divorce: Mark 10:1-12 Reconsidered." *Journal of the Evangelical Theological Society.* 25:3, September 1982.

Heth, William A. and Gordon J. Wenham. *Jesus and Divorce: The Problem with the Evangelical Consensus.* Nashville: Thomas Nelson, 1985.

Honea, Sterling R. *Love, Sex, Marriage and Divorce.* Los Angeles: California Lawyers Press, 1980.

Howell, John C. *Equality and Submission in Marriage.* Nashville: Broadman Press, 1979.

Joiner, E. Earl. *A Christian Considers Divorce and Remarriage.* Nashville: Broadman Press, 1983.

Kysar, Myrna. *The Asundered, Biblical Teachings on Divorce and Remarriage.* Atlanta: John Knox Press, 1978.

Laney, J. Carl. *The Divorce Myth.* Minneapolis: Bethany House, 1981.

_____. "Paul and the Permanence of Marriage in 1 Corinthians 7." *Journal of the Evangelical Theological Society.* 25:3, September 1982.

Lewis, Alvin, Ed. *A Consultation on Marriage, Divorce and Remarriage.* National Association of the Church of God and The

National Board of Christian Education of the Church of God. West Middlesex, Pa., 1979.

Luck, William F. *Divorce and Remarriage: Recovering the Biblical View.* New York: Harper and Row, 1987.

Montefiore, Hugh. *Remarriage and Mixed Marriages: A Plea for Dual Reform.* London: Society for the Publication of Christian Literature, 1967.

Olsen, Viggo Norskov. *New Testament Logia on Divorce: A Study of Their Interpretation from Erasmus to Milton.* Tubigen, Mohr Siebeck, 1970.

Petersen, James A. *Two Become One.* Wheaton: Tyndale House, 1973.

Plekker, Robert J. *Divorce of the Christian: What the Bible Teaches.* Wheaton: Tyndale House, 1989.

Shaner, Donald W. *Christian View of Divorce According to the Teachings of the New Testament.* Leiden, J. Brill, 1969.

Small, Dwight Hervey. *The Right to Remarry.* Old Tappan, N.J.: Fleming H. Revell Co., 1975.

Smalley, Stephen S. Edited by I. Howard Marshall. "Redaction Criticism." *New Testament Interpretation.* Grand Rapids: William E. Eerdmans Publishing Co., 1977.

Smith, David Lorne. "A Theology of Divorce and Remarriage." Dissertation. Louisville, KY: Southern Baptist Seminary, 1984.

Stein, Robert H. "Is It Lawful for a Man to Divorce His Wife?" *Journal of the Evangelical Theological Society.* June 1979.

Stott, John R. W. *Divorce.* Phillipsburg, N.J.:

Presbyterian and Reformed Press, [1960,] 1972.

Thielecke, Helmut. John W. Doberstein, transl. *Theological Ethics.* Vol. 3: "Sex." Grand Rapids: William E. Eerdmans Publishing Co., 1964.

Warner, Daniel S. *Marriage and Divorce.* Grand Junction, Mich.: Gospel Trumpet Co., n.d.

Washington, Cecil M. *The Truth about Divorce and Remarriage.* Nappanee, IN., Evangelical Publishing House, 1957.

Yankelovich, David. *New Rules: Searching for Self-Fulfillment in a World Turned Upside Down.* New York: Random House, 1981.

Yarborough, O. Larry. *Not Like the Gentiles, Marriage Rules in Paul.* Chico, Ca.: Scholars Press, 1986.

Articles published in *The Gospel Trumpet* by the Gospel Trumpet Co., Anderson, Ind.

Byers, Jacob. W. "Deceived and Deceiving." Oct. 31, 1985.

Byrum, E. E. "Strange Leadings." Nov. 8, 1894.

Fisher, Joseph C. "The Law of Christ Concerning Marriage." March 1, 1885.

_____. "Pernicious Doctrines." Oct. 4, 1894.

Schell, W. G. "Divorce in Paul." June 8, 1899.

Warner, D. S. "Answers to Questions," Jan. 11, 1894.

_____. "Answers to Questions," August 8, 1895.

_____. "Not Yet Delivered," Feb. 15, 1888.

_____. "Is God's Grace Too Strong For You?" Dec. 20, 1894.

Wyrick, N. "An Explanation." Jan. 15, 1894.